D0912279

The Cooperative Classroom: Social and Academic Activities

Jacqueline Rhoades

and

Margaret E. McCabe

National Educational Service

Bloomington, Indiana 1992

Copyright 1992 by
Jacqueline Rhoades
and
Margaret E. McCabe

All rights reserved, including the right of reproduction
of this book in whole or in part in any form.

Cover design by Kris Coates

Cover illustration by Amanda Bowlen

Cover and chapter illustrations by
Broadview Elementary sixth graders
Bloomington, Indiana

Printed in the United States of America

recycled paper

ISBN 1-879639-16-5

About the Authors

JACQUELINE RHOADES received her BA in Sociology and MS in Education with a minor specializing in work with mentally retarded students. She has held positions as a special education teacher, a reading program coordinator, a staff development trainer for the California State Department of Education. She currently works as a program specialist in a K-12 unified school district, a professional development consultant, and as an adjunct professor in teacher education.

MARGARET E. McCABE has a BA and MS in psychology and an Ed.D. in Education Management. She has worked as a school psychologist, director of state and federal projects, a public information officer, school principal, superintendent, program reviewer for the California State Department of Education, vocation expert for national health and welfare department. Currently, she is a part-time university professor in teacher and administrator preparation programs. She is also a professional development consultant and writer.

Peggy and Jacquie are frequent speakers at major national and international conventions and have provided training workshops for thousands of teachers and administrators over the last several years in a variety of topic areas including but not limited to cooperative learning, social skills development, developing higher order and critical thinking skills, managing productive meetings, and stress and time management.

A Message from the Authors:

We are sometimes asked how we came about developing this cooperative learning model we call "Simple Cooperation."

We have each been using various forms of cooperation with students for more than twenty years. We have also been teaching our students how to communicate more effectively and how to get along with others. When we first began presenting our ideas in cooperative learning workshops, we didn't think about it in terms of a "model." We believed that direct instruction in specific social skills, such as communication, problem solving, conflict management, group dynamics and meeting management needed to be included in the daily curriculum—in a deliberate and continuous manner.

We were also addressing the questions most workshop participants asked: "What social skills do I begin teaching first?" and "Exactly how do I teach them?" Our response was to identify the specific social skills necessary for success in and out of school, to describe and explain each of those skills, to create a social skills continuum to be used as a guide, and to develop various activities to teach and practice each skill. Our goal was, and is, to make the process of teaching and learning these skills simple, thus the term "Simple Cooperation." Notice, we said *simple;* it is not necessarily easy but the rewards are well worth the effort.

At least one of us has used every activity and technique in this book. We hope you and your students will enjoy using these ideas as much as we do. If you develop an activity or process that works well and that you'd like to have printed, send it on to us. We'll include it with your name in a future book.

Peggy & Jacquie

Table of Contents

Introduction 1

○ Chapter 1
Opening, Getting Acquainted, Making Transitions, and Energizing 3

☆ Chapter 2
Enhancing Social Awareness and Self-Esteem 21

△ Chapter 3
Enhancing Communication Skills. 35

✓ Chapter 4
Enhancing Problem-Solving Skills 59

✸ Chapter 5
Enhancing Thinking Skills 71

✪ Chapter 6
Wrapping Up. 91

✐ Chapter 7
Activities Across the Curriculum 99

❖ Chapter 8
Breaking Up 121

✳ Chapter 9
Jigsaw Variations. 127

Appendix A
Student Grouping Techniques. 139

Appendix B
Awards and Forms 149

Introduction

We are asked at least a couple of dozen times a month to write a cooperative activities book emphasizing social skills development. The following pages reflect our efforts to fulfill that request. You may recognize some of the activities from *Simple Cooperation in the Classroom* and *The Nurturing Classroom* (and even from our workshops) but many of the exercises and ideas that follow are new.

The activities included in this book follow the same general pattern found in the *Simple Cooperation* model. For that reason, we decided it would be helpful to say a few words about this approach.

The illustration on the next page reflects the inter-relationship of the components of the simple cooperation model. The development of thinking skills permeates all activities; every lesson, every exercise is an opportunity to develop alternate thinking paths, to develop higher order complex thinking skills. Developing thinking skills is never forgotten; it is an essential part of this model.

Simple cooperation approaches instruction of social skills in a sequential, deliberate manner. Rather than teaching the specific social skill needed for today's lesson or worse, assuming students will gain these skills as a side effect of the group process, the simple cooperation model incorporates specific social skills as a part of the curriculum.

Building self-esteem, while not reflected in the illustration, is a major component of most cooperative learning models. Enhanced self-esteem is generated through successful group processes, through meeting management techniques, and through carefully thought-out reward systems. The old adage "Success breeds success" is certainly true and cooperative activities set students up for success. In many instances, students would have to work hard to not succeed.

The first day of school can be an anxiety-provoking experience for many students, especially those who are new to the school. Taking the time for students to become acquainted with you and with each other will set a positive tone for the classrooms and develop group cohesiveness more quickly which, in turn, will promote an accelerated degree of learning both social skills and academic content. *Getting Acquainted* activities are carefully structured to dispel some of the anxiety students may be feeling and to promote acceptance and understanding between and among teacher and students.

Two other types of activities closely related to *Getting Acquainted* activities are *Openings* and *Transitions*. *Opening Activities* are used at the beginning of the school day. They help students develop a "mind set" for the day. Certain *Getting Acquainted* activities can also be used as Openers such as: "What we have in common," "Similarities" and "Focus Worksheet."

Transition Activities are used after lunch in elementary grades and at the beginning of the class period in secondary schools. When students are away from the group, their thoughts are diverted from the group goal; it's important to help them refocus their minds and energies on that group goal. At the elementary level or in any self-contained classroom, use transition activities after recess, after lunch and between the end of one subject area and the beginning of another.

At the secondary level, as students move from class to class, say from a science class to a literature class, the English teacher tends to expect students to be thinking about whatever piece of literature they're studying as soon as they enter the room. This is an unrealistic expectation especially if the student was involved in some fascinating experiment in the science class. The student's thoughts are still on that experiment. A *Transition* activity will help that student "leave" the science class and begin thinking about literature. At the secondary level, either an opening or a transition activity needs to be used to begin the class period.

Energizers are another type of activity used in the cooperative classroom. As the name implies, these activities are used when students are "fading"—when energy is low, when it's too warm, when any students seem especially tired or are having trouble concentrating. The *Energizer* is a quick activity to "wake students up."

The following are samples of these four kinds of activities.

Introductions

GRADE LEVEL: Kindergarten – Adult
GROUP SIZE: 2
ROLES: None
TIME: 20 – 35 minutes
MATERIALS: Directions written on chart paper or on the chalkboard
PURPOSE: Getting Acquainted—use at the beginning of the year and when new students are enrolled in your class
ACTIVITY: Students will each interview a partner, then each will introduce the other to the class using the information obtained during the interview.

1. Decide what questions students will use in the interview. The number and complexity of questions will depend upon your grade level, the attention span of your students and the time available for the activity. Questions might include things like: name, hobby, favorite TV show, number of brothers and sisters, place of birth, etc.

2. Write the questions on large chart paper or chalk board.

3. Students choose a partner — a person they don't know or, at least, a person they don't know well.

4. Students "interview" each other for three to five minutes each, obtaining the specified information.

5. At the end of the time period, each student introduces his partner to the class.

Self-Description

GRADE LEVEL: 2 – Adult
ROLES: None
TIME: 15 – 20 minutes
MATERIALS: Paper and pencil
PURPOSE: Getting Acquainted or Opening
ACTIVITY: Students write a description of themselves. Teacher collects the descriptions and reads them aloud one at a time; class guesses who is being described.

VARIATION: Conduct in small group setting with a group "Reader" sharing the information for everyone in the group. The entire class would still guess who in each group is being described.

The Adjective Name Memory Game

GRADE LEVEL: 3 – Adult
ROLES: None
TIME: 20 – 30 minutes
MATERIALS: None
PURPOSE: Getting Acquainted, Opening, or Energizer
ACTIVITY:

1. The class, including the teacher, sits in a circle.

2. Students, beginning to the right of the teacher, recite the alphabet in sequence, each student saying only one letter of the alphabet.

3. The sound of the letter each student says becomes the beginning sound of an adjective the student chooses to describe herself, example, Affable Jane, Bouncy Mary, etc.

4. Give students one to two minutes to think of an adjective.

5. Then, students take turns, again beginning with the student to the immediate right of the teacher, introducing themselves by adjective and first name.

VARIATIONS:

a. After going around the circle, repeat the process with the added task of stating the names of students who have already introduced themselves. Example:

   Jane, the first student on the teacher's right, will say only her adjective and name, "Affable Jane." Mary, the next student, would say, "Affable Jane, Bouncy Mary." The third student would say, "Affable Jane, Bouncy Mary, Cute Jamie." And so on around the circle.

b. Allow students to the immediate right and left of the speaker help by whispering answers when the speaker forgets.

c.   Students select adjectives that have the same initial sound or letter as the initial letter/sound in their first name.

NOTE: You may wish to seat students you know have short term memory deficits to your immediate right. This will avoid placing these students "on the spot" by requiring them to remember more names than they may be capable of.

Guess That Person

GRADE LEVEL: 3 – Adult
ROLES: None
TIME: 10 minutes, additional time during day, and 10 minutes at end of day
MATERIALS: One index card or piece of paper per student and pen/pencil
PURPOSE: Getting Acquainted, Opening Transition or Energizer
ACTIVITY:

1.   On an index card or piece of paper, write one thing about yourself you think nobody knows.

2.   Hang the cards or papers on a wall.

3.   During the day, everyone reads the descriptions and writes below them who they think the person is.

4.   At the end of the day, read each card and the guessed identities.

5.   The real person identifies himself or herself.

What We Have in Common

GRADE LEVEL: 4 – Adult
GROUP SIZE: 4 – 5
ROLES: Recorder and Time-Keeper
TIME: 10 – 20 minutes
MATERIALS: Paper and pencils
PURPOSE: Getting Acquainted, Opening, Transition, Energizer
ACTIVITY:

1. Assign students to groups of 4 or 5.

2. Teacher suggests categories of possible commonalities and gives examples.

3. Within groups, students discuss possibilities.

4. Group members then determine three things they have in common.

5. Each group's recorder shares with the rest of the class the commonalities found within his group.

    A discussion about what students learned through this activity is a nice wrap up.

Similarities and Differences

GRADE LEVEL: K – Adult
GROUP SIZE: 2 – 4
ROLES: Recorder
TIME: 10 – 15 min.
MATERIALS: Paper, pencils and measuring instruments (e.g. ruler, yardstick)
PURPOSE: Getting Acquainted, Opening – use at the beginning of the year or day
ACTIVITY:

1. Place students in groups of two to four.

2. Appoint a Recorder for each group. The recorder will also be the spokesperson for the group.

3. Give students a list of characteristics or facts to compare and contrast among group members, i.e. to find what is similar and what is different, such as: tallest/shortest; longest/shortest foot; shortest/longest hair; longest/shortest fingers (or index finger or thumb or little finger) ; biggest/smallest hand; longest/shortest arm.

4. Groups gather information within the allotted time.

5. Groups share their results with the rest.

VARIATIONS:

For Math classes:

a. Students can convert linear measurements to metric.

b. Students can devise a formula to express the differences within their groups.

For Language Arts classes:

Students can write a narrative describing similarities and differences within their group.

Self-Description

GRADE LEVEL: 2 – Adult
ROLES: None
TIME: 10 -15 minutes
MATERIALS: Paper and pencil/pen
PURPOSE: Getting Acquainted or Opening
ACTIVITY:

1. Each student writes a description of himself.

2. Teacher collects the descriptions and reads them aloud one at a time to the rest of the class.

3. Class guesses who is being described.

VARIATION: Conduct in small groups and assign a "reader" in each group. The "reader" will read the descriptions of the students in the group. The rest of the class guesses who in the group is being described.

Self-Portrait

GRADE LEVEL: K – 4
ROLES: None
TIME: 15 – 20 minutes
MATERIALS: Paper and pencil/crayons/pens
PURPOSE: Getting Acquainted or Opening — use at the beginning of the year or day

ACTIVITY:

1. Students draw a picture of themselves.

2. Teacher collects and attaches to wall.

3. During the day, students look at pictures and guess who the person is by writing that person's name under the picture.

4. At the end of the day, have a "to tell the truth" time; each student identifies which picture is his or hers.

VARIATION: Each student draws a picture of their hand by tracing it. Teacher collects and attaches to wall. Students guess whose belongs to each hand.

Friendly Aliens are Arriving

GRADE LEVEL: 2 – 6 (This can be used in secondary and adult classes)
GROUP SIZE: 3 – 5
ROLES: Recorder
TIME: 15 – 20 minutes
MATERIALS: Paper and pencil/pen
PURPOSE: Opening – use at beginning of day

ACTIVITY:

1. Assign students to group.

2. Appoint a Recorder for each group.

3. Tell students this story: "We have finally had communication with intelligent life forms from another galaxy. They want to visit Earth. Their planet is very different from ours. The people all look alike but they have the ability to make themselves look like anyone. They want us to send them descriptions of Earth-people so that they can "fit in" to our

world. Our class has been asked to write detailed descriptions for these people. They will then make themselves look like our descriptions before they arrive on Earth."

4. Each group is then instructed to write a detailed description of human being. Impress upon your students that this is serious and they are not to write descriptions of horror figures, rather, the description should be a combination of how each person in the group looks.

5. At the end of the time, each group reads their description to the rest of the class.

One Fact

GRADE LEVEL: Preschool – Adult
ROLES: None
TIME: 20 – 25 minutes
MATERIALS: None
PURPOSE: Getting Acquainted or Opening – use at the beginning of the year or day
ACTIVITY: Students are seated randomly in a circle and instructed to tell one fact they have learned this year about the person on their right. The only restriction is that it must be a positive statement about the person.

You will lead the activity by stating one new fact you have learned about the person on your right then the process is continued around the circle until the student on your left tells one new fact he or she has learned about you.

Getting Acquainted Cards

GRADE LEVEL: 2 – Adult

GROUP SIZE: 3 – 4

ROLES: None

TIME: 20 – 25 minutes

MATERIALS: Name tags or 3 x 5 index cards (pins or tape are needed if index cards are used), directions and sample Getting Acquainted card written on chart paper or chalk board.

PURPOSE: Getting Acquainted or Opening – use at the beginning of the year or day and when new students are enrolled in your class

ACTIVITY: Each student is given a name tag or index card and is instructed to write her first name in the center. Students then complete their name tag by following the instructions written on the sample.

You can help students by verbally "walking" them through the activity. Examples:

- In the upper right hand corner, write the location of your last vacation.

- In the lower right hand corner, write the number of your brothers and sisters.

- In the lower left hand corner, write the name of your favorite TV program.

- In the upper left hand corner, write the name of the city where you were born.

The completed *Getting Acquainted* card is attached to the writer's shirt or blouse. The class is then divided into groups of three or four. Group members share the information on their Getting Acquainted card.

VARIATION: This can be done in pairs, larger groups or with the entire class.

Sample Getting Acquainted Card

City where born	Last vacation place
	Name	
Favorite TV program	Number brothers/sisters

Completed Getting Acquainted Card

San Jose	Disneyland
	Elaine	
Star Trek	1 brother, 2 sisters

The Whip

GRADE LEVEL: Preschool – Adult

ROLES: None

TIME: 10 minutes

MATERIALS: None

PURPOSE: Transition or Energizer

ACTIVITY: Students are asked to formulate a one word response to an open-ended question, e.g. "A one word description of how I am feeling this moment is...." Students are given a minute or two to think of their response.

Beginning with one student, "whip" around the room rapidly giving each student the opportunity to respond or "pass." Regardless of student response, simply say "thank you" and go on to the next student.

Students must be given the option to pass, i.e., not respond directly to the question, because some may not be able to think of an answer and others may feel threatened by the question. Students may also want to test you to see if you really mean it's okay to say "I pass" rather than offer how they are feeling, thinking, etc.

Focus Worksheet

GRADE LEVEL: 2 – Adult
ROLES: None
TIME: 10 – 20 minutes
MATERIALS: A prepared worksheet on which five to ten questions have been listed. The questions may be academic, social, trivia or a combination thereof. (See Figure 4.)
PURPOSE: Getting Acquainted, Opening, Transition
ACTIVITY:

1. A worksheet is distributed to each student with instructions to complete the worksheet by interviewing fellow students.

2. Students may not obtain more than one answer per student.

3. A specific amount of time is given to complete the activity, such as five or ten minutes, depending upon the complexity and number of questions.

Be prepared for lots of movement and a relatively high noise level.

At the end of the activity, you may wish to have students turn in the worksheets, share the information they have gained in a small group, or discuss each question with the entire class.

This activity is excellent for reviewing material, preparing students for a test, reinforcing specific data or information you consider important, and getting better acquainted with each other.

Sample Focus Worksheet

Instructions
1. Find someone who can correctly answer the following questions or who fits the description.
2. Have that person sign in the appropriate place.
3. Each question/description should be signed by a different person.

1. Explain Opening Activities:_____

2. Give an example of a Wrap-Up activity _____

3. Someone wearing blue _____

4. What is the purpose of Getting Acquainted Activities? _____

5. Someone born in this city _____

6. When would you use a Transition Activity? _____

The items on the Focus worksheet can be meant as a review of material recently covered in class or they can all focus on getting acquainted. Even when the Focus Worksheet is used for review, some non-academic questions should be scattered throughout.

It does not matter how many items are included; there can be as few as three or as many as twenty. Obviously, the more items, the longer it will take students to complete.

Guess That Number

GRADE LEVEL: 2 – Adult
ROLES: None
TIME: 10 – 20 minutes
MATERIALS: Name tags on which random numbers between 1 and 1,000 are written. Adjust the range of numbers according to your students' ability level. For grade 2, for instance, you might only include numbers between 1 and 50. Instructions are written on the chalkboard or on large chart paper hung on the wall.
PURPOSE: Opening, Transition
ACTIVITY: The object is for each student to discover his number.

1. Numbered name tags are placed on students' backs.

2. Students may not see their own number.

3. Students discover their number by asking other students any of the following questions:

   a. Is my number lower than....?

   b. Is my number higher than....?

   c. Is my number ....?

   d. Responses may be "yes" or "no."

4. As students walk around the room they ask each other any of the three questions.

They may not ask two consecutive questions of the same person. Example:.Jamie may ask Maria, "Is my number higher than 50?" Maria may answer with a "yes" or a "no." Jamie must then ask another student one of the three questions.

5. When a student discovers his number, he returns to his seat.

6. At the end of the allotted time period, all students return to their seats. Students who have not yet discovered their numbers may elect to continue the game during recess or break time, or they may be told their numbers.

VARIATION: Use the alphabet, vocabulary words, mathematical equations, science facts, or any other facts you want to reinforce.

Exercises

GRADE LEVEL: Preschool – Adult
ROLES: None
TIME: 5 Minutes
PURPOSE: Energizer
ACTIVITY: Lead your students in various physical exercises such as stretching, bending, jumping jacks, walking in place, etc., as appropriate for your grade level. (This is one of our favorites when people start getting tired and/or to begin the day.

VARIATION: Lead the class in a game of "Simon Says." This works especially well if you are teaching in tight quarters. Examples include: "Simon says touch your nose." "Simon says touch your left shoulder with your right thumb."

Bees

GRADE LEVEL:	Kindergarten – Adult
ROLES:	None
TIME:	1 – 2 minutes
MATERIALS:	None
PURPOSE:	Energizer
ACTIVITY:	All group members mimic the sound of bees (zzzzzzz) beginning very softly and gradually increasing in loudness.

Applause

GRADE LEVEL:	Preschool – Adult
ROLES:	None
TIME:	15 – 30 seconds
MATERIALS:	None
PURPOSE:	Energizer
ACTIVITY:	Students simply applaud for about 15 seconds.

Chapter 2

Enhancing Social Awareness and Self-Esteem

Jennifer Smith

Alone or Lonely – Which Is Which?

GRADE LEVEL: 5 – 12
GROUP SIZE: 3 – 4
ROLES: Recorder and Spokesperson
TIME: 10 – 15 minutes.
MATERIALS: Paper and pencil
PREPARATION: Teacher leads a class discussion on what it means to be alone and what it means to be lonely.

ACTIVITY:

1. Assign students to groups.

2. Appoint a Recorder and Spokesperson for each group.

3. Students decide if there is a difference between being alone and being lonely. Allow about 5 – 7 minutes for this discussion.

4. Spokesperson shares group's thoughts.

Privacy

GRADE LEVEL: 4 – 12
GROUP SIZE: 3 – 4
ROLES: Recorder and Spokesperson
TIME: 10 – 20 minutes
MATERIALS: Paper and pencil
PREPARATION: Teacher leads a class discussion on the definition of "privacy." What is privacy? and What do people do to indicate they need privacy?

ACTIVITY:

1. Assign students to groups.

2. Appoint a Recorder and Spokesperson for each group.

3. Students write one paragraph telling why people in general may sometimes need privacy and when and why they themselves sometimes need privacy. Allow about 10 – 12 minutes for students to discuss and write paragraph.

4. Spokesperson shares group's thoughts.

Temper

GRADE LEVEL: 3 – 12

GROUP SIZE: 3 – 4

ROLES: Recorder and Spokesperson

TIME: 10 – 15 minutes

MATERIALS: Paper and pencil

PREPARATION: Teacher leads a class discussion on "losing your temper" with students brainstorming a list of the types of things that cause them to lose their tempers. Also discuss the results of losing one's temper — "Does it accomplish anything?" Write list on chalkboard.

ACTIVITY:

1. Assign students to groups.

2. Appoint a Recorder and Spokesperson for each group.

3. Students list as many options they can think of to use instead of "losing their temper."

4. Spokesperson shares group's thoughts.

Kindness

GRADE LEVEL: 3 – 12

GROUP SIZE: 3 – 4

ROLES: Recorder and Spokesperson

TIME: 10 – 15 minutes.

MATERIALS: Paper and pencil

PREPARATION: Teacher leads a class discussion on kindness; if possible, include a current newspaper article depicting a kind act. Have students participate in defining "kindness."

ACTIVITY:

1. Assign students to groups.

2. Appoint a Recorder and Spokesperson for each group.

3. Students list as many acts of kindness that they have observed in the past week. Allow about 5 minutes for the group discussion.

4. Spokesperson shares group's thoughts.

More Alike Than Not

GRADE LEVEL: 3 – 8

GROUP SIZE: 3 – 4

ROLES: Recorder and Spokesperson

TIME: 10 – 15 minutes

MATERIALS: Paper and pencil

PREPARATION: Teacher leads a class discussion on how we often focus on the differences in people but in reality people are more alike than different.

ACTIVITY:

1. Assign students to groups.

2. Appoint a Recorder and Spokesperson for each group.

3. Students list as many ways they can think of that people, in general, are alike. Examples: all people need to breathe, drink water, eat food, have feelings, have abilities, etc. Allow 5 – 7 minutes for this discussion.

4. Recorder writes group's responses.

5. Spokesperson shares group's thoughts.

Write a Dictionary

GRADE LEVEL: 2 – 8

GROUP SIZE: 3 – 4

ROLE: Recorder

TIME: 10 – 15 minutes.

MATERIALS: Paper and pencil

PREPARATION: Teacher selects a social skill he or she wants to emphasize such as friendship, clear communication, giving compliments. Teacher also leads a discussion on the dictionary emphasizing words and definitions.

ACTIVITY:

1. Assign students to groups.

2. Appoint a Recorder and Spokesperson for each group.

3. Students write a "dictionary" that contains words relevant to the selected social skill topic.

4. Recorder writes group's "dictionary."

5. Students sign their dictionary to indicate their agreement with its contents.

6. Teacher collects dictionaries and places them where everyone can read them.

Courage

GRADE LEVEL: 2 – 8
GROUP SIZE: 2 – 3
ROLES: Recorder and Spokesperson
TIME: 10 – 15 minutes
MATERIALS: Paper and pencil
PREPARATION: Teacher selects and reads newspaper article, short story or essay that relates a courageous act.

ACTIVITY:

1. Assign students to groups.

2. Appoint a Recorder and Spokesperson for each group.

3. Groups write a definition of courage and list any acts of courage they have seen. Allow about 5 – 7 minutes for this discussion.

4. Spokesperson shares group's thoughts.

Criticism

GRADE LEVEL: 3 – 12
GROUP SIZE: 3 – 4
ROLES: Recorder and Spokesperson
TIME: 10 – 15 minutes
MATERIALS: Paper and pencil
PREPARATION: Teacher leads a class discussion on criticism — what is "criticism," what is the difference between criticizing people and criticizing things or ideas.

ACTIVITY:

1. Assign students to groups.

2. Appoint a Recorder and Spokesperson for each group.

3. Groups discuss and decide responses to these questions: "Is criticism ever good?" "Why/why not?" Allow 5 – 7 minutes for discussion.

4. Spokesperson shares group's responses.

The Cold Shoulder

GRADE LEVEL: 3 – 12
GROUP SIZE: 3 – 4
ROLES: Recorder and Spokesperson
TIME: 10 – 15 minutes
MATERIALS: Paper and pencil
PREPARATION: Teacher leads a class discussion defining the term, "the cold shoulder."

ACTIVITY:

1. Assign students to groups.

2. Appoint a Recorder and Spokesperson for each group.

3. Groups list as many reasons they can think of for people "giving you the cold shoulder." allow 5 – 7 minutes for discussion.

4. Recorder writes group's responses.

5. Spokesperson shares group's thoughts.

FOLLOW-UP: Have groups write a paragraph on how it feels to receive the "cold shoulder."

Good Job!

GRADE LEVEL: 2 – 5
GROUP SIZE: 3 – 5
ROLES: Recorder, Timekeeper and Spokesperson
TIME: 10 – 15 minutes
MATERIALS: Paper and pencil
ACTIVITY:

1. Assign students to groups.

2. Appoint a Recorder, Timekeeper and Spokesperson for each group.

3. Groups brainstorm, in three minutes, as many ways they can think of to say "good job!"

4. Recorder writes group's responses.

5. Spokesperson shares group's list.

I Know the Answer

GRADE LEVEL: 3 – 12
GROUP SIZE: 3 – 4
ROLES: Recorder and Spokesperson
TIME: 15 – 20 minutes
MATERIALS: Use a problem completed in any subject area. Word and logic problems are especially challenging.

ACTIVITY:

1. Assign students to groups.

2. Appoint a Recorder and Spokesperson for each group.

3. Groups discuss, in detail, the steps necessary to complete the problem.

4. Recorder writes group's answer.

5. Spokesperson shares group's response.

"I Feel Hurt!"

GRADE LEVEL: 3 – 12

GROUP SIZE: 3 – 4

ROLES: Recorder and Spokesperson

TIME: 10 – 15 minutes

MATERIALS: Paper and pencil

PREPARATION: Teacher leads a brief class discussion defining "feeling hurt" and why people try to protect themselves from feeling hurt.

ACTIVITY:

1. Assign students to groups.

2. Appoint a Recorder and Spokesperson for each group.

3. Groups list as many ways they can think of that people protect themselves from feeling hurt.

4. Spokesperson shares group's list.

VARIATION: Make a class list on chalkboard and discuss how people may interpret the behaviors listed. For example....if a person withdraws in order to protect themselves from feeling hurt, some people might think they aren't friendly.

...But How Do I Begin a Conversation...

GRADE LEVEL: 3 – 6

GROUP SIZE: 2

ROLES: "Old Timer" and "New Student"

TIME: 5 – 10 minutes

MATERIALS: Chairs

LEAD-IN: Have students imagine they are new to the school. Discuss how it feels to be new and know no one.

ACTIVITY:

1. Assign students to groups.

2. Have "Old Timer" sit on chair in an imaginary cafeteria.

3. Have "New Student" enter and sit down beside the "old timer" and try to begin a conversation.

4. Switch roles.

5. Conduct class discussion on how it felt to be both the "old timer" and the "new student."

What Makes a Friend

GRADE LEVEL: 2 – Adult

GROUP SIZE: 3 – 4

ROLES: Recorder and Spokesperson

TIME: 10 – 30 minutes

MATERIALS: Paper and pencil/pen

PREPARATION: Teacher leads a general class discussion about friendship – what friendship is and the fact that we each look for some of the same qualities in a friend but we each may look for different qualities or certain characteristics may be more important to one person than to another. Write key words that evolve from discussion on chalk board.

ACTIVITY:

1. Assign students to groups of 3 – 4.

2. Assign Recorder and Spokesperson for each group.

3. Each group discusses the characteristics and personal qualities they would like to have in a friend.

4. Each group reaches a consensus decision on three or four qualities or characteristics.

5. The group recorder writes these qualities.

6. Group Spokespersons read their answer to the class.

FOLLOW-UP: Teacher leads a discussion acknowledging similarities and differences between and among groups' responses and pointing out that it's okay that each person is different — there is no right answer.

Acceptance

GRADE LEVEL: 4 – 6

GROUP SIZE: 3 – 4

ROLES: Recorder and Spokesperson

TIME: 5 – 10 minutes

MATERIALS: Paper and pencil/pen

PREPARATION: Teacher leads a discussion on the definition of "acceptance," including students' meaning of what acceptance is.

ACTIVITY:

1. Assign students to groups of 3 – 4.

2. Have groups write a list of qualities or characteristics they find hard to accept.

3. Spokesperson from each group shares the group's response at the end of the allotted time.

4. Teacher leads a class discussion exploring why acceptance of differences is often difficult for people of all ages. Have students generate a list of benefits gained from adopting a more accepting attitude.

Worry

GRADE LEVEL: 3 – 6

GROUP SIZE: 3 – 4

ROLES: Recorder and Spokesperson

TIME: 15 – 20 minutes

MATERIALS: Paper and pencil/pen

PREPARATION: Teacher leads a discussion on "worry" — what is it; what kinds of things do we worry about. It is important to generate a list from the students themselves.

ACTIVITY:

1. Assign students to groups of 3 – 4.

2. Have groups write two to four paragraphs about what happens to an issue or situation when you worry about it (e.g., it seems bigger than life; it feels like it's overwhelming; all our energy is consumed on this one issue or situation, etc.)

3. Spokesperson from each group reads his or her group's "report."

4. Teacher leads class discussion on alternatives to worrying.

Apologizing

GRADE LEVEL: 2 – 12
GROUP SIZE: 2
ROLES: Recorder and Spokesperson
TIME: 30 – 40 minutes
MATERIALS: Paper and pencil/pen
PREPARATION: Teacher leads a discussion on the definition of "apologizing," and when an apology is appropriate.

ACTIVITY:

1. Assign students in groups of 2.

2. Assign the Recorder and Spokesperson for each pair.

3. Students develop a role-play demonstrating an apology. Give students five minutes to prepare their role-play.

4. Each pair is then given up to 3 minutes to role-play their apology for the class.

5. Class discusses how their role-plays felt and how they think they would feel actually apologizing to someone.

FOLLOW-UP: It is important for the teacher to lead a discussion focusing on how to accept an apology gracefully.

Write a Recipe

GRADE LEVEL: 2 – 8

GROUP SIZE: 3 – 4

ROLES: Recorder and Spokesperson

TIME: 10 – 20 minutes

MATERIALS: Paper and pencil/pen

PREPARATION: Teacher selects a topic area relevant to a social skill that he or she wants to reinforce such as clear communication, making or being a friend, saying thank you, giving or receiving a compliment, etc.

ACTIVITY:

1. Assign students to groups of 3 – 4.

2. Each group writes a recipe for the skill selected.

3. The Spokesperson for each group reads the recipe to the class.

Chapter 3

Enhancing Communication Skills

Tiffaney Allgood

The following activities reinforce effective sending and receiving skills. Some relate directly to being a successful sender, others focus on being a successful listener, while still others enhance nonverbal messages. While it's possible to give an exclusive nonverbal message, it is not possible to send an exclusively verbal message — there are always nonverbal cues attached, e.g., tone of voice. For this reason many of the following activities will reinforce speaking, listening, and nonverbal messages simultaneously.

Definitions

GRADE LEVEL: 3 – 12

GROUP SIZE: 3 – 4

ROLE: Recorder and Spokesperson

TIME: 10 – 15 minutes

MATERIALS: Teacher selects a word or phrase relevant to the social or academic curriculum such as clear communication, cooperation, justice, etc.

ACTIVITY:

1. Assign students to groups of 3 – 4 members each.

2. Appoint Recorder and Spokesperson for each group.

3. Tell students the selected word or phrase.

4. Each group develops a definition for the word or phrase.

5. Spokesperson shares his or her group's definition.

6. Discuss differences and how different interpretations of the same word can lead to miscommunication.

What's in the News — A Practice in Summarizing

GRADE LEVEL: 3 – 12

GROUP SIZE: 3 – 4

ROLES: Recorder, Reader and Spokesperson

TIME: 10 – 15 minutes.

MATERIALS: Newspaper article

PREPARATION: Select a current newspaper article and duplicate one copy for each group.

ACTIVITY:

1. Assign students to groups.

2. Appoint a Recorder, Reader and Spokesperson for each group.

3. Reader reads article to the group.

4. Groups develop a 1 to 3 sentence summary, as appropriate for the article.

5. Recorder writes group's summary.

6. Spokesperson shares group's thoughts.

VARIATION: Each group receives a different article.

Accepting and Receiving Compliments

GRADE LEVEL: K – Adult

GROUP SIZE: 2

ROLES: None

TIME: 5 minutes

PREPARATION: Teacher leads a class discussion on compliments. During the discussion compliments should be defined. A list of complimenting phrases should be elicited from the students and written on the board, such as: "I like....," "good idea," "that was great," and so on. A discussion on how to receive compliments is also conducted. Write a list of responses to receiving and accepting compliments such as: "thank you," "how nice of you to notice," "I'm glad you appreciated what I did," "that makes me feel good," and so on.

ACTIVITY:

1. Pair students.

2. One student compliments his partner who, in turn, responds.

3. Switch roles.

Telling it Straight

GRADE LEVEL: 3 – 12

GROUP SIZE: 2

ROLES: Speaker and Listener

TIME: 10 – 15 minutes

PREPARATION: Teacher conducts a class discussion on the importance of sending clear messages. Discuss how miscommunication can occur if the message is confused. Tell students "we are now going to practice telling it straight." Select a topic relevant to the curriculum such as: describing the sun move across the sky; the changes in an egg as it fries; how the pupil of the eye dilates, etc.

ACTIVITY:

1. Pair students.

2. Students decide who will be the first speaker.

3. The speaker verbally describes the selected topic to the listener.

4. Switch roles.

5. Students discuss what they could do to send a clearer message next time. Discuss what difficulties, if any, they encountered.

6. Pairs share their insights.

What's in the Box?

GRADE LEVEL: 3 – 8
GROUP SIZE: 4 – 5
ROLES: Speaker and Guessers
TIME: 5 – 10 minutes
MATERIALS: Individually selected
PREPARATION: Teacher selects one speaker for each group. The speaker selects an object and places it in a box. The speaker's group does not know what the object is.

ACTIVITY:

1. Assign students to groups.

2. The speaker describes the object in the box to his group. She can discuss uses, size, shape, color, etc.

3. The group may not ask questions about the object.

4. The speaker continues giving clues until the guessers correctly identify the object.

The Unfair Grade

GRADE LEVEL: 3 – 8
GROUP SIZE: 2
ROLES: "Teacher" and "Student"
TIME: 5 – 10 minutes
PREPARATION: Teacher discusses how there are times when teachers may make mistakes grading a paper OR there may not be a mistake but the student believes there is one. The truth of the matter can only be revealed through open communication.

ACTIVITY:

1. Pair students.

2. Pairs decide who will role play the teacher first.

3. "Student" approaches "teacher" with a concern regarding a grade received on a paper that the "student" believes is unfair. This time the "teacher" has indeed made a mistake. Allow 2 – 3 minutes for this interaction.

4. Switch roles.

5. "Student" approaches "teacher" with a concern regarding a grade which she believes is unfair. In this instance, the teacher has not made a mistake.

The Unwanted Gift

GRADE LEVEL: 2 – Adult
GROUP SIZE: 2
ROLES: None
TIME: 5 – 10 minutes
PREPARATION: Teacher discusses with the class that sometimes people may want to give us gifts that we do not need or want. This puts us in an awkward place if we take the gift — we won't use it and that may hurt our friend's feelings. To avoid the problem we can tell our friend in some way (that does not hurt his or her feelings) that we would rather not have this particular item.

ACTIVITY:
1. Pair students.

2. Each student practices gracefully sending the message that they do not want the intended gift. For example, say you guessed or learned that your friend was going to give you a specific shirt that you did not need or want. You might try to include your feelings about that shirt in a conversation that you were having.

3. Following the role play, pairs describe how they felt during the activity.

Paraphrasing Verbal Messages

GRADE LEVEL: Grade 2 – Adult
GROUP SIZE: 2
ROLES: None
TIME: 10 – 15 minutes
MATERIALS: None

The Verbal Map

GRADE LEVEL: Kindergarten – Adult
GROUP SIZE: 2
ROLES: None
TIME: 10 – 20 minutes
MATERIALS: None

ACTIVITY:

1. One student, the speaker, gives verbal directions from the classroom to the office, rest room, playground or some other campus location.

2. The second student, the listener, may use clarifying techniques, then follows the directions exactly as given.

3. Upon returning, the listener reports whether or not he actually arrived at the desired location.

Follow this activity with a discussion about what went right and wrong, pointing out the necessity for clarity when speaking and clarifying when listening.

VARIATIONS:

a. Allow the listener to take notes when directions are being given.

b. Listener may not use clarifying techniques. The activity then focuses primarily on clear message sending.

The Unknown Design

GRADE LEVEL: Kindergarten – Adult

GROUP SIZE: 2

ROLES: None

TIME: 10 – 15 minutes

MATERIALS: A geometric design drawn by the teacher; paper and pencils for students.

ACTIVITY: The design is drawn and placed outside the visual range of students, such as the back side of a portable chalkboard or behind a room divider.

1. One student is selected to be the "director." She verbally instructs the class to individually reproduce the given design on the paper provided to them.

2. The students, "artists," may not ask the "director" any questions.

3. After the "director" has completed giving directions, she shows the design to the "artists." They, in turn, compare their drawings with the original design.

4. The last step is for you to lead a discussion related to the experience asking such questions as: "What did the 'director' say that helped you reproduce the design?" "Why were some 'artists' successful in reproducing the design and others not successful?"

VARIATION: Conduct activity in pairs, one person being the "director," the other, the "artist."

Geometric Design Samples

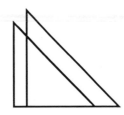

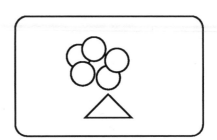

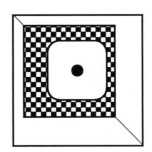

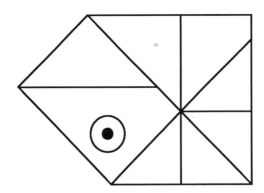

Tangrams

GRADE LEVEL: 2 – Adult

GROUP SIZE: 3 – 5

ROLES: Facilitator as Monitor; Optional – Observer

TIME: 15 – 20 minutes

MATERIALS: Tangram packets for each group of students. Packets contain the pieces for five separate tangrams of three pieces each. See next page for sample tangrams.

ACTIVITY:

1. Establish groups of three to five students each, depending on grade level.

2. Appoint a Facilitator as Monitor for each group.

3. Distribute packet of materials to the Facilitator of each group.

4. Facilitator distributes the 15 pieces one at a time to group members in same manner as dealing out a deck of cards. Some group members may have more pieces than others.

5. The group then begins the task of solving the puzzle, i.e., putting the four squares together from the pieces.

RULES:

a. No speaking or sounds of any sort.

b. Students communicate with each other by trading and moving tangram pieces until the four squares are made.

c. Students should be told that their tangram pieces will make squares of identical size.

VARIATION: For Grades 5 – Adult, the role of Observer may be included in this activity. An observer would be appointed for each group. Behaviors to be observed could include: following directions; cooperation/sharing of pieces; nonverbal messages being used and/or what process the group used to complete the task.

Sample Tangrams

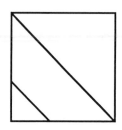
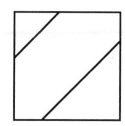

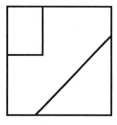
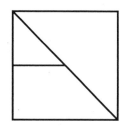
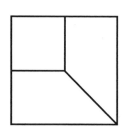

Giving Directions

GRADE LEVEL: 3 – Adult

GROUP SIZE: 2

ROLES: None

TIME: 10 – 15 minutes

MATERIALS: Direction cards showing cubes in different patterns; patterned cubes or blocks

ACTIVITY: Students are grouped in dyads. Object is for one student to give the other nonverbal directions to assemble a pattern with the cubes or blocks.

1. First student has activity card (be sure partner does not see card), second student has cubes/blocks.

2. Student #1 gives nonverbal directions to student #2.

3. Allow 3 – 5 minutes for the activity, then have student #2 look at direction card and compare to his design.

4. Reverse roles.

5. Discuss the degree of success students experienced; what contributed to this success; and how directions can be given nonverbally to allow others to follow them.

Find the Feeling

GRADE LEVEL: Kindergarten – Adult

GROUP SIZE: 2 – 3

ROLES: None

TIME: 10 – 15 minutes

MATERIALS: Anything displaying pictures of people, e.g., magazines, newspapers.

ACTIVITY: In small groups of two or three, students are instructed to find all the pictures reflecting a specific feeling such as: happy; worried; confused; sad; excited, etc.

Identify the Feeling

GRADE LEVEL: Kindergarten – Adult

GROUP SIZE: 2 – 3

ROLES: None

TIME: 5 – 10 minutes

MATERIALS: Pictures of people

ACTIVITY: In groups of two or three, students are given two pictures of people exhibiting different emotions/feelings and are asked to identify what they think the people are feeling.

IDEA: Use cartoon or "smiley" faces for primary age children.

Music Is My Business

GRADE LEVEL: Preschool – Adult

ROLES: None

TIME: 5 – 10 minutes

MATERIALS: Prerecorded tape or phonograph record with appropriate playing machine.

ACTIVITY:

1.   Play music to class.

2.   Discuss with students — "the way the music makes me feel."

3.   Play the same selection again; students may dance around classroom reflecting the way the music makes them feel.

Literature and Feelings

GRADE LEVEL: Kindergarten – Adult
GROUP SIZE: 2
ROLES: None
TIME: 30 – 60 minutes
MATERIALS: The Rotten Chicken; drawing paper; crayons
ACTIVITY: Read The Rotten Chicken aloud to class. A specific discussion question is then presented to students. Students are divided into dyads (two students per group) and instructed to do the following:

1. Decide how to depict the group's feeling response to the question.

2. Draw a group picture representing the feeling response to the question; all students must participate in the drawing.

3. If group members disagree about how to depict the feeling in the drawing, this should be reflected in the drawing.

Sample Questions to ask class:

● How do you act when you feel rotten?

● How does it feel when you believe in yourself?

● How did the willow tree feel after it helped the hen?

● How did the young rooster's feelings change about himself and his mother?

After the pictures are completed, they may be posted on the bulletin board or used as a kick-off for further discussion.

NOTE: The Rotten Chicken is a modern allegory and may be interpreted on many levels. While written in a format appropriate for children, the story line inherently includes themes of adult complexity, among which is psychological abuse.

This title is offered as an example of the use of literature in listening skills activities. Select titles that will be most appropriate for your class. Some criteria to consider when selecting stories for this activity:

a. Story should be brief, taking no longer than 10 minutes to read.

b. Story should contain a message that elicits a feeling response.

c   It is extremely beneficial when the author has provided discussion questions – this will decrease preparation time.

Mirroring

GRADE LEVELs: Kindergarten – Adult
GROUP SIZE: 2
ROLES: None
TIME: 6 – 8 minutes
MATERIALS: None
ACTIVITY: This is a fun activity that enhances nonverbal anticipation. It also dramatically demonstrates the difference between leaders and followers.

1. Students choose partners and stand facing each other.

2. One partner is designated the leader, the other is the "mirror."

3. The leader makes a series of movements, which are followed as closely as possible by the "mirror."

4. After two to three minutes, switch roles.

5. Discuss how students felt in each role.

NOTE: Initially, students will need to be directed to begin with slow movements to give the "mirrors" a fair chance to imitate with ease.

VARIATION: When first beginning this activity, it may be helpful for primary grades to have the teacher be the leader, with all students mirroring the teacher.

Music Interpretation

GRADE LEVEL: 3 – Adult

GROUP SIZE: 3 – 4

ROLES: None

TIME: 15 – 30 minutes

MATERIALS: Prerecorded tape or phonograph record

ACTIVITY:

1. Assign students to groups of three or four.

2. Students are instructed to listen to the musical selection (suggested length: 2 – 3 minutes) and, as a group, develop a nonverbal interpretation of the music.

3. The group product is limited to two to three minutes and may be performed with the music as a direct interpretation or without the music as an indirect interpretation.

4. Groups perform for the class at the end of their planning time. Planning time can be 5 – 15 minutes during which time, it will be helpful to have the music playing softly in the background. The interpretation could take the form of a dance, pantomimed skit or any variation thereof.

Expression!

GRADE LEVEL: 3 – Adult

ROLES: None

TIME: 20 – 40 minutes

MATERIALS: 4 x 6 index cards. A specific feeling/emotion is written on each card, such as happy, disgusted, worried, confused, excited, etc. At least 20 different feelings are needed.

ACTIVITY: Place cards face down on a desk or table.

1. Students take turns drawing a card (don't let anyone else see the card) and acting out the feeling that is written on their card. It will be helpful to place a time limit of two or three minutes on each demonstration.

2. The rest of the class guesses what feeling is being demonstrated.

3. At the end of each student's turn, he or she shows the class what feeling is written on the card.

4. The card is then placed at the bottom of the stack.

VARIATION: Conduct activity in small groups of four or five students each.

Becoming Aware of Your Nonverbal Messages

GRADE LEVEL: 6 – Adult
GROUP SIZE: 2
ROLES: None
TIME: 10 – 15 minutes
MATERIALS: None
ACTIVITY:

1. In pairs, students tell each other how they "know" the other one is happy, sad, excited, embarrassed, angry or whatever feelings you specify.

2. The receiver/listener affirms or denies that is what she is actually feeling when she demonstrates that nonverbal action.

3. When both students have had the opportunity to share their perceptions with feedback, have a class discussion about how easy it is to misinterpret another person's nonverbal messages, and the importance of checking out our perceptions.

On Becoming a Poet

GRADE LEVEL: 2 – Adult
GROUP SIZE: 2
ROLES: None
TIME: 15 – 25 minutes
MATERIALS: One piece of paper and pencil for each student.
ACTIVITY:

1. Each pair decides who will be "A" and who will be "B."

2. Without looking at each other's paper, the "A" students write their greatest wish or fantasy; while the "B" students write the most perfect place, activity, or circumstance they can think of.

3. Pairs read their "poem" aloud to the class, hearing it for the first time themselves: "A"s read their part first, followed immediately by "B."

Sample Poem:

"A" – "I would like to be floating on clouds in the sky."

"B" – "Eating chocolate ice cream."

On Becoming an Actor

GRADE LEVEL: 2 – Adult
ROLES: None
TIME: 15 – 20 minutes
MATERIALS: Charted poem or tongue twister at an appropriate reading level for your students; 15 – 3 x 5 index cards with one emotion or feeling written on each one, e.g., happy, sad, angry, excited, dull, brave, surprised, etc.
ACTIVITY: The poem or tongue twister written on a chart pad or chalkboard must be placed within easy view for all students. Sample tongue twister:

Sister Susie sits by the Sea Shore Sewing Skirts (or sifting sand or selling sea shells).

1. The deck of emotion/feeling cards is placed on a table or desk.

2. Students take turns going to the front of the room, drawing a card (no one else should see the card).

3. Student demonstrates the emotion or feeling while reading the poem or tongue twister. Demonstration of the feeling can be done with intonation, volume, facial expression, and body language.

4. Other students attempt to identify the emotion/feeling being demonstrated.

VARIATION: Students may be divided into smaller groups of 3 – 6; each group is given a stack of index cards with a feeling written on each one.

How to Be a Good Listener

GRADE LEVEL: Kindergarten – Adult
GROUP SIZE: 3
ROLES: Speaker and Listener
TIME: 20 – 30 minutes
MATERIALS: None
ACTIVITY: This activity has four distinct parts. Begin by grouping students into triads. Each triad decides who will be "A," "B" and "C."

PART 1: Experiencing "Plops" – a "plop" happens when someone says something and the listener(s) do not acknowledge the comment.

1. "B's" and "C's" leave the room or congregate at the far end of the room. They will be the "listeners" and are instructed to pay no attention to the speaker. Instead, they are to look around the room, doodle, and/or pick up and scan through a book. It's important that the "A's" do not hear these instruction.

2. Instruct "A's" to discuss their favorite activity, what they did over the weekend, or any other topic appropriate to the age group.

3. Reestablish the triads and direct them to begin the activity. You can only allow one or two minutes for the "A's" to try to get their message across.

PART 2: Experiencing disinterest — Change roles. "B's" become the speakers.

1. "A's" and "C's" are instructed to demonstrate lack of interest by checking their watch or clock, yawning, looking at speaker, then looking away.

2. Instruct "B's" to discuss a topic appropriate to their age level, anything will do such as: "how to be a friend."

Again, stop the activity after one to two minutes.

PART 3: Experiencing attentiveness — Switch roles. "C's" become the speakers.

1. Instruct "A's" and "B's" to demonstrate effective listening behaviors.

2. Instruct "C's" to discuss what animal they like best and why, or any other topic appropriate to age level.

PART 4: Class Discussion

1. Following the activities, ask how students felt in each situation.

2. Discuss how important listening techniques are in any discussion or conversation.

SOURCES:

Becoming Aware: Mary Rose, Teacher, Ukiah, Calif.

On Becoming An Actor and Expression!: Marvin Roupe, Teacher, Point Arena, Calif.

On Becoming A Poet: Ann Marie Samson, Teacher and Poet, Willits, Calif.

News Reporter: Adapted by Jacquie and Peggy from the "old" telephone gossip game. Original source unknown.

Tangrams; The Unknown Design: Original source unknown.

Chapter 4

Enhancing Problem-Solving Skills

Sina Kramer

The following problem solving model can be modified to use with any situation that requires a solution. It is as valuable in academic lessons as it is in social situations. In other words, this model can be used when Cindy and Mike are quarreling about whose turn it is to be group Praiser or it can be used by a social studies group to plan ways of completing a major research project.

There are nine steps in this problem solving model. It is not necessary to include each step with every problem.

The Steps

1. **State the problem.** Write it down, just as you perceive it. Example: two students fighting.

2. **Identify the components of the problem.** Before you can resolve a problem, you need to identify and analyze its component parts, such as: who and what is affected by the "problem"; when does it occur; who's involved. This step provides greater clarity of the problem situation and often results in valuable clues for resolving it.

   For example, when two students are arguing, have each write down how they perceive the problem and how it might be resolved.

   This step helps diffuse emotionality and starts to give you the information necessary for an effective solution.

3. **Determine what you want to happen instead of what's happening.** Example: "Students to settle disagreements through discussion rather than physical or verbal assault." Most of the time, your students will be able to identify behaviors that would be more effective in settling disputes. Once in a while, you may need to offer suggestions or help them generate a list of alternative actions.

4. **Redefine the problem and state it as a question.** This step requires you to analyze the information gathered in the previous three steps. After you have identified and reviewed the components and how you want the situation to change, you will have a clearer idea of what the issues really are. At this time, you will probably find it helpful to redefine the problem and to state it as a question. Example: "How can Jack

and Marie settle their disagreement without fighting?" Fisticuffs or verbal assault are certainly disallowed behaviors, but the real issue may be that neither student knows any other way to resolve differences.

5. **Identify the constraints.** Constraints are factors outside the problem itself that have an impact on the solution to the problem. Among the constraints to be considered are: time – by when must the problem be resolved? resources – what resources, e.g., money, materials, are available for resolving the problem? politics or social norms – what community or school rules must be considered when determining a solution? Example: district or school policy requires suspension for any student involved in a physical fight; obviously, students must learn how to resolve their differences without hitting each other.

6. **Specify the final decision maker and what decision making model will be used.** Will the decision be made by consensus? By democratic vote? By the teacher? By the principal? By the board? Example: students and teacher must arrive at a consensus decision on how to resolve these two students' differences.

7. **Brainstorm possible solutions.** Once the problem has been defined, the constraints clearly identified, the final decision maker and decision making mode specified, possible solutions are brainstormed. Everyone involved in the problem should be included in the brainstorming process. This is a time to share all ideas, without judgment.

   As an example, our fighting students might brainstorm this list:

   - not play together
   - sit in office during recess
   - kick the other kid out of school
   - learn a different way to settle disagreement

8. **Evaluate the possible solutions in light of the constraints and in terms of their feasibility and probability for success.** Following the brainstorming session, compare each idea against the list of constraints. Using a matrix like the one shown is an easy and effective way to determine which ideas fall within the constraints.

The next step is to examine each idea that meets the constraints in terms of feasibility and probability for success. With our fighting students, "not playing with each other" may meet the constraints but it has a low probability of success because it doesn't change anything. Eventually, these two students will interact on the playground, in the hall, etc.

9. **Select and implement a solution.** Since it was previously determined that teacher and students must reach a consensus decision, it would be up to them to decide which of the possible solutions will be implemented.

Once the solution has been selected, it is critical to clearly outline who will do what, when it will be done, and when and how the solution will be evaluated to determine its degree of success.

This becomes the implementation plan and should be written and signed by everyone involved. For example, if our fighting students agreed they would prefer to learn different ways in which to handle their differences, the agreement might look like this:

AGREEMENT BETWEEN JACK AND MARIE

1. Jack and Marie agree they will not hit, push or shove each other.
2. Jack and Marie agree to learn how to handle their differences by sitting down and talking about them with Ms. Johnson.
3. Ms. Johnson agrees to help Marie and Jack learn how to solve their differences by discussing exactly what each one thinks and feels until they reach a mutual understanding.
4. Jack, Marie and Ms. Johnson will meet again in one week on (month and date) to reevaluate this agreement.

Signed:

_____

_____

_____

Date:

_____

The 1st Step in Teaching Problem Solving: Brainstorming

At first glance, the concept of brainstorming seems simple: generate as many ideas as possible within a given amount of time and do not evaluate the ideas while you are brainstorming. In reality, implementing the most important rule, no evaluation, is very difficult to do. Why? Because it means that you cannot say things like, "great idea!" "yea" "oh, that's good" or give any nonverbal judgments such as nodding, grunting or other guttural sounds.

People in general, and teachers in particular, like to reinforce, or at least acknowledge, another person's comments and contributions. It's very hard to not do this.

The second issue in brainstorming is the temptation to immediately begin discussing the pros and cons of an idea or to make comments such as: "We've tried that already" or "There's not enough money for that," etc.

One technique to use when first learning brainstorming is to have a nonparticipating member designated as a "flagger." The "flagger" sits or stands outside the group and literally throws a flag (a nerf ball, handkerchief or some other piece of material) into the group when members wander off into discussion or evaluation.

The last major difficulty with brainstorming is that people are still hesitant to offer ideas they consider "farfetched." In fact, some individuals are just shy about offering any idea, believing their ideas are not as good as some others. It takes time and lots of encouragement to eliminate these fears. It also takes time and practice to dust off some of the creative cobwebs. With persistence and actualization of the "safe and secure" classroom promise, your students will all eventually join in a lively and enthusiastic brainstorming session.

The Future

GRADE LEVEL: 2 – Adult
GROUP SIZE: 3 – 5
ROLES: Grades 4 – Adult, use Advanced Facilitator and Recorder; in primary grades, teacher acts as Facilitator
MATERIALS: Chalkboard or large chart paper and marking pens
ACTIVITY: The idea is to brainstorm what something will be like in the year 2000, or any year in the future.

The purpose of this activity is to simply gain experience brainstorming and to allow oneself to be creative.

Ideas:

Transportation	Schools
Games and Sports	Stores
Television and Movies	Work
Homes	Government
Heating and Cooling Systems	Computers

Anything you can think of!

Creative Uses

GRADE LEVEL: 3 – Adult
GROUP SIZE: 3 – 5
ROLES: Advanced Facilitator and Recorder
TIME: 10 – 15 minutes
MATERIALS: Large chart paper and marking pens, OR use chalkboard
ACTIVITY: Using almost anything found in a classroom, generate ideas about how it can be used aside from its general use.

Examples:

Chalkboard eraser	Ruler
Pencil eraser	Paper clips
Chalk	Computer disc
Pencils	Stapler

After the brainstorming session, the facilitators share their respective groups' ideas with the rest of the class.

The Inkless Pen

GRADE LEVEL: 4 – Adult

GROUP SIZE: 3 – 6

ROLES: Advanced Facilitator and Recorder

TIME: 10 – 15 minutes

MATERIALS: Felt tip water color marking pens and large chart paper hung on the wall OR use chalk board

ACTIVITY: Groups of 3 – 6 students are formed, depending upon grade level. An Advanced Facilitator and Recorder are selected for each group. (Note: if using groups of 3, the Facilitator and Recorder will participate in the brainstorming. If using groups of 5 or 6, they will not participate.)

Tell the following story:

"A company has one million felt tip marking pens and they don't know what to do with them — they forgot to put the ink in them. They don't want to throw them away because they will lose thousands and thousands of dollars. We have to think of how we can use these no-ink pens."

Each group brainstorms as many ideas for using the pens as they can within four minutes. Teacher acts as time-keeper. Remember to give students a minute or two thinking time before the actual brainstorming begins.

At the end of the brainstorming session, each Facilitator shares the group's ideas with the class.

NOTE: Ideas generated from various groups have included such things as: baby's toy, sell as invisible ink pens, mobiles, new kind of toy boat or missile, take the felt out and use as tooth pick holders.

Cooperative Problem-Solving Activities

The following three problem solving activities all use the same process. These kinds of activities are powerful in terms of developing higher order thinking skills, in developing alternative thinking paths, in enhancing metacognition and in mediating problem-solving strategies.

GRADE LEVEL: 7 – Adult

GROUP SIZE: 4 – 5

ROLES: Facilitator and Recorder

TIME: 45 minutes

MATERIALS: Packet of clues for each group.

PREPARATION: Write clues on index cards as indicated below. You'll need one packet for each group.

ACTIVITY:

1. Assign students to groups.

2. Appoint a Recorder and Facilitator for each group.

3. Have Facilitator from each group get a packet of clues for his or her group. Facilitator then distributes the clues as you would deal a deck of playing cards.

4. Group solves problem.

5. Recorder writes group's response and how they arrived at their conclusion.

6. When groups think they have the answer, they raise their hands. Teacher goes to group and tells them if their responses are correct or incorrect. If correct, group must assure every member knows how to solve the problem. If not, members who know how to solve problem "teach" process to others. If everyone in group knows how to solve problem, group members may act as coaches for groups who have not completed the problem. Coaches do not tell the answer — they guide the other group's members through the process.

7. Allow about 30 minutes for groups to solve the problem.

8. Wrap-up: Groups discuss how they approached the problem, i.e., what strategy did they use.

9. Groups share their strategies.

Cooperative Problem 1

PROBLEM SITUATION:

Four women — Sarah, Joan, Rose, and Elaine — met at a mutual friend's luncheon. They had met once before but did not really know each other. Their mutual friend thought they would like each other and sat them at the same table for lunch. For reasons only they understood, they were not willing to tell very much about their respective husbands. In fact, of the statements each made the only thing for certain is that the statement in which a woman mentions her own husband's name is correct.

After reading the clues, determine who is married to whom.

Margaret Smythe: Trevor is Scott's father.
I have never met Anthony.

Joan Carson: Rose's husband is either Trevor or Anthony.
Scott is the oldest.

Rose Jones: Anthony is Margaret's husband.
Trevor is Scott's older brother.

Elaine Redding: Rick is my son.
Trevor is older than my husband.

1. Write the introduction to the problem on a card.

2. Write each statement with the name of its speaker on a separate card.

3. The Introduction and each statement makes a packet.

   ANSWER: Rick Smythe
   Anthony Carson
   Trevor Jones
   Scott Redding

Cooperative Problem 2

PROBLEM SITUATION:

During a tour of Europe, a student from the American Cooperative University found herself rooming at a hostel with three other college students, each from a different country. Among them, they spoke four languages: English, Spanish, Swedish and Russian. Even though each woman could speak two of four languages there was not one language in which they could all converse. In fact, only one of the languages was spoken by more than two of the students.

Study the clues and determine which two languages each woman spoke.

- Nobody spoke both Spanish and Swedish.

- Tina couldn't speak English but she could act as interpreter for Rachel and Patty.

- Patty spoke Swedish. She could talk with Paula but Paula did not know any Swedish.

- Tina, Rachel, and Paula did not speak the same language.

1. Write the Introduction to the problem on a card.

2. Write each clue on a separate card.

3. The Introduction and each clue go together to make a packet.

ANSWER: Patty spoke Swedish and Russian.
Tina spoke Spanish and Russian.
Rachel spoke English and Spanish.
Paula spoke English and Russian.

Cooperative Problem 3

PROBLEM SITUATION:

The Jenkins family dominates both the social and "political" life in the small community of Gardner. Currently, five of the family members (Mr. & Mrs. Jenkins, their daughter, Mr. Jenkins's sister, and Mrs. Jenkins's mother hold the powerful positions of general store owner, mayor, School Board president, County Council representative, and principal in this small town.

Study the clues and determine which family member holds which position.

● The mayor and the principal are not blood relatives.

● The general store owner is younger than her brother-in-law but older than the principal.

● The County Council representative was captain of the debate team in college. The County Council representative is older than the School Board president.

ANSWER: Mr. Jenkins is the principal.

Mrs. Jenkins is the mayor.

Jenkins's daughter is the School Board president.

Mr. Jenkins's sister is the general store owner.

Mrs. Jenkins's father is the County Council representative.

Chapter 5

Enhancing Thinking Skills

Travis Sutherlin

Cooperative learning inherently enhances the development of higher order thinking skills; however, teachers can use activities to focus on specific thinking skills. The following activities are designed to increase students' thinking paths thereby offering each student alternative ways of thinking about various problems and situations.

What Is Thinking?

GRADE LEVELS: 3 – 12

GROUP SIZE: 3 – 4

ROLES: Recorder and Spokesperson

TIME: 5 – 15 minutes

MATERIALS: Paper and pencil/pen

ACTIVITY:

1. Assign students to groups of 3 – 4.

2. Appoint the Recorder and Spokesperson.

3. Each group writes a definition of "thinking." Student should consider what they do when they think, how they know they're thinking; how they might know someone else is thinking; how someone else might know they are thinking; and any behavioral characteristics that would be evident when someone is thinking.

4. Students sign answer sheet to indicate agreement with group response.

5. Spokesperson from each group reads the group response.

FOLLOW-UP ACTIVITY:

Groups note the similarities and differences between and among the different responses.

What's in an Advertisement?

GRADE LEVEL: 3 – 12

GROUP SIZE: 3 – 4

ROLE: Recorder and Spokesperson

TIME: 10 – 20 minutes

MATERIALS: Paper, pen/pencil, advertisements cut out of magazines and/or newspaper. One advertisement per group is needed.

PREPARATION: Teacher leads a class discussion about magazine and newspaper advertisements touching on what qualities really sell a product. For example....a fast-food restaurant may be promoting friendship.

ACTIVITY:

1. Assign students to groups of 3 – 4.

2. Distribute advertisements to groups.

3. Instruct students to analyze the advertisement and list what they think the "real" sales feature are. What emotions or characteristics are the advertisements promoting.

4. The group's recorder writes the group's response.

5. The spokesperson from each group shows the class the advertisement and reads the group's answer.

"Advertisement for Us"

GRADE LEVEL: 3 – 8
GROUP SIZE: 3 – 4
ROLES: Recorder
TIME: 15 – 20 minutes
MATERIALS: Paper, pencil and colored marking pens
PREPARATION: Teacher leads a discussion about the purpose of advertisements and how advertisers "sell" their products. Generate from the class advertising-type words.

ACTIVITY:

1. Assign students to groups of 3 – 4.

2. Appoint the Recorder for each group.

3. Each group is to write an advertisement about their group listing the selling points. They may illustrate their advertisement in whatever way they think will enhance the important features about the group.

4. Hang up their advertisements on the wall.

The Crystal Ball

GRADE LEVEL: 3 – 12
GROUP SIZE: 3 – 4
ROLES: Recorder and Spokesperson
TIME: 10 – 15 minutes
MATERIALS: Paper and pencil/pen
PREPARATION: Teacher selects a topic relevant to the curriculum – examples: transportation, ecology, world peace, technology, scientific discoveries, etc. Teacher then discusses crystal balls and the fact that some people believe they can see into the future. Finally, select a future time period, e.g., 10 years in the future, 100 years in the future.

ACTIVITY:

1. Assign students to groups of 3 – 4.

2. Assign the Recorder and Spokesperson for each group.

3. Each group is to "look into" their imaginary crystal ball and to forecast what the specific topic area will look like at that time period. Example: Transportation — 100 years from now, we'll travel on people movers. There won't be any automobiles as we know them, instead there will be heliocars, magnetic transport movers, and so on.

4. Spokesperson for each group shares group's responses.

VARIATION: Students can enhance forecast by drawing a picture.

A Good Idea?

GRADE LEVEL: 3 – 8
GROUP SIZE: 3 – 4
ROLE: Recorder and Spokesperson
TIME: 10 – 15 minutes
MATERIALS: Paper and pencil/pen
PREPARATION: Teacher leads a class discussion on inventions, famous scientific discoveries, or relevant creative ideas.

ACTIVITY:

1. Assign students to groups of 3 – 4 members each.

2. Appoint Recorder and Spokesperson for each group.

3. Students discuss and decide how they know they or someone else has a "good idea." Give students 5 minutes to reach their decision.

4. Spokesperson shares group's response.

Rent it for a Day

GRADE LEVEL: 3 – 12
GROUP SIZE: 3 – 4
ROLE: Recorder and Spokesperson
TIME: 10 – 15 minutes
MATERIALS: Paper and pencil/pen
PREPARATION: Teacher selects a characteristic, quality, or attribute relevant to the academic or social skills curriculum such as: brains, personality, attitude, etc.

ACTIVITY:

1. Assign students to groups of 3 – 4 members.

2. Appoint Recorder and Spokesperson for each group.

3. Each group completes the following statement: "If we could, we would rent (person's name)'s (quality/attribute/characteristic) because _____. Example: "If we could we would rent President Lincoln's Brain because he figured out how to win the Civil War.

4. Spokesperson shares group's response with rest of class.

Making it Happen

GRADE LEVEL: 3 – 12
GROUP SIZE: 3 – 4
ROLE: Recorder and Spokesperson
TIME: 15 – 30 minutes
MATERIALS: Paper and pencil/pen studied.
PREPARATION: Teacher selects a topic area relevant to current curriculum area or community life such as: world peace treaty, building a health clinic in your town, putting a traffic light at the intersection near the school.
Teacher then leads a discussion on selected topic.

ACTIVITY:

1. Assign students to groups of 3 – 4 members.

2. Introduce the selected topic.

3. Groups develop a plan to "make it happen."

4. Spokesperson for each group shares his group's plan.

FOLLOW-UP DISCUSSION:

What can students do to affect change in their school or community?

Can You Remember?

GRADE LEVEL: 2 – 12
GROUP SIZE: 2 – 4
ROLES: Recorder and Spokesperson
TIME: 10 – 15 minutes
MATERIALS: Worksheet
PREPARATION: Prepare a worksheet which includes questions regarding the school environment. Example:

1. How many secretaries work in the school office?

2. How many hopscotch patterns are on the playground?

3. How many gates are there to the school yard?

4. How many trees are there in the school yard?

5. How many classrooms are in this wing?

ACTIVITY:

1. Assign students to groups.

2. Appoint a Recorder for each group.

3. Distribute one worksheet to each group.

4. Recorder writes group's responses.

5. Spokesperson shares his or her group's responses.

6. Conduct discussion about observing environment.

Peanut Butter & Jelly Sandwich— Exactly as You Say

GRADE LEVEL: 3 – Adult
GROUP SIZE: 3 – 4
ROLES: Recorder and Spokesperson
TIME: 15 minutes
MATERIALS: Paper, pen/pencil, bread, peanut butter, jelly, knife
ACTIVITY:

1. Assign students to groups and appoint Recorder and Spokesperson for each group.

2. Recorder writes down directions for making a peanut butter and jelly sandwich. Emphasize that it is important to leave nothing out; each step of the process needs to be written clearly and specifically. Tell students that the Spokesperson will read the directions to you and that you will follow those directions exactly.

3. Give students 10 minutes to write their directions to make the sandwich.

4. Spokesperson from each group, one at a time, reads group's directions. You follow directions exactly as stated. For example, if students have neglected to write "open the jar of peanut butter" and the first direction is to "put knife in jar" — you would follow the direction, bumping the knife on the jar lid. Caution...this can get messy!

5. Complete the activity by having groups discuss what worked and what didn't within their directions.

Envision the Abstraction

GRADE LEVEL: 3 – 12
GROUP SIZE: 2 – 3
ROLES: None
TIME: 15 – 20 minutes
MATERIALS: Paper, pencil, crayons or marking pens
PREPARATION: Select an abstract concept relevant to the academic or social skill presently being taught. Conduct a class discussion about the concept, including topics such as definition, how you recognize the concept in "real life," how you recognize the concept yourself. Examples of concepts: justice, faith, friendship, conscience, power, values, creativity, acceptance, sense of humor, democracy.

ACTIVITY:

1. Assign students to groups.

2. Select a concept.

3. Students work together to draw a picture of the concept.

NOTE: It is a good idea to give 5 minutes discussion/think time before students begin drawing.

---

4. Collect and attach drawings to bulletin board.

5. Class discusses differences and similarities between and among drawings.

Do They Really Have Anything in Common?

GRADE LEVEL: 3 – 12

GROUP SIZE: 3 – 4

ROLES: Recorder and Spokesperson

TIME: 15 – 20 minutes

MATERIALS: Paper and pencil

PREPARATION: Teacher chooses two objects or events relevant to current curriculum.
Example of objects: vase and glass, apple and orange; Train and airplane; tree and deer.
Example of events: 1980 and 1988 presidential campaign.

ACTIVITY:

1. Assign students to groups.

2. Appoint Recorder and Spokesperson for each group.

3. Instruct student to list all the thinks the two objects or events have in common.

4. Recorder writes group's responses.

5. Spokesperson shares group's responses.

VARIATION: Have students complete Venn diagram listing characteristics or qualities two objects/events have in common and those they do not have in common.

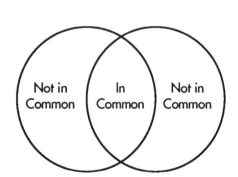

Sample

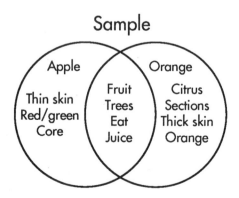

The following quick instructions/activities will enhance thinking skills within the group process. These suggestions will also help students prepare for a more successful cooperative group experience.

1. Give students "think time" before the group begins the task. Instruct students to individually think about how they will approach the task or problem for one minute before the group begins discussion.

2. Instruct group to develop a strategy before beginning the task.

3. Instruct the group to discuss the importance of the content before beginning the assignment.

4. Have the group talk about when, why, and how the information contained in the task is to be used.

5. Have the group review the questions and identify what is to be learned.

The following list of activities will enrich the mediation process. These activities foster self-awareness of thinking strategies and provide a mechanism for sharing internal dialogue with others.

While the mediation process occurs naturally in cooperative groups, you can broaden and enrich the process by planning group activities to encourage the sharing of internal dialogue.

1. Include concrete examples and tasks in group activities. For example, provide materials such as newspaper and paper clips, and instruct students to develop a plan for building the tallest tower possible and follow that plan to build the tower. The plan must be developed within a given amount of time (around 10 minutes). Only after the plan is completed my the building begin and students must build exactly as planned. This forces "thinking before doing."

2. Discuss the meaning of words. For example, have groups agree on a common definition of the word "surplus" when discussing government subsidy in relation to farming.

3. Have groups verbally "walk through" the thinking strategies they used in finding a solution to a problem.

4. Practice brainstorming. Have groups brainstorm as many ideas as they can for using an object in a way that is different than its intended use. Any object will work — pencils, chalk, erasers, paper clips, and so on.

5. Ask groups to generate questions for a passage they have just read.

6. Ask groups to determine how many different ways the quality of a lesson can be evaluated. For example, how many factors could be graded in an English composition or a term paper.

7. Have students paraphrase sections of required reading passages. In other words, they would write the meaning of the passage in their own words.

8. Synthesize reading material. After reading an assignment, each group would write what they determine to be the essence of the material in the fewest words possible.

9. Students can explore and discuss the consequences of their behavioral choices. Examples: "What happens if I don't complete my homework?" "What are the consequences if I decide to take drugs?"

10. Self-evaluation. Group members are asked to evaluate their social or academic performance in the group.

11. Giving feedback. Groups are asked to share their reaction to the information you present in the lesson.

12. Sharing points of view. Groups are required to develop a point of view about a current political event and to share it with other groups. (Or, individuals within each group share their points of view with each other.)

13. Role playing. Each group is assigned a specific behavior or social skill to "role play" for the other groups.

14. Elaborate on an idea. After hearing or reading a concept, each group must expand on the idea and write as much as they can that directly relates to the concept.

15. Discuss "what if..." For example, have groups discuss: "What if the South had won the Civil War?"

16. Describe how objects or events relate to each other. Examples...how does learning to read relate to future income; or, how does our national deficit relate to the value of the dollar; or, how does a penny relate to a nickel.

17. Placing events in sequential order. Almost any content area can be used: provide students with a mixed up list of the daily schedule and have them rearrange it to reflect the class schedule; present the major wars in which the U.S. has been involved and require them to list the wars in sequential order.

18. Relate past and present to future, such as: how will learning the Pythagorean theorem today be useful in the future, as adults?

19. Predict the future. Examples include: envisioning what school will be like in 2005. Expand on this by having groups draw or build a model of what the school would look like, or what transportation vehicles might look like.

20. Identify the pros and cons of current issues, such as listing reasons why they should or should not vote for specific political candidates.

The following are examples of Wrap-Up activities which will promote the development of effective thinking strategies: enhance metacognition; ensure sharing of internal dialogue; and provide mediation.

Wrap-Ups place a demand on the group and the individuals within the group to be aware of their own internal dialogue and to share that with others. The Wrap-Up can be a powerful activity in helping students establish effective thinking strategies.

Have students discuss each of the following either in their cooperative group or in a whole class discussion.

1. After completing this assignment, one question I have is...

2. I can use the information I learned today in the future by...

3. One way I contributed to my group was...

4. One new thing I learned was...

5. I disagree with _____ because...

6. A better title for this book is...

7. I felt the greatest strength of the character in this story was...

8. If _____ had happened, the outcome of the story would have been...

9. I discovered _____ in this lesson.

10. I disagree with the author about _____ because...

11. If I had written this story, I would have...

12. If I had lived in that time era, I would feel...

13. If I were _____, I would...

14. I am concerned about...

15. If I were (a particular figure in history or character in a story), I would have...

16. One frustration I felt during this activity was...

17. One good feeling I had during this activity was....

18. I received help from my group in....

19. If we were to do this activity again, I would suggest...

20. Our strategy for accomplishing this task was...

21. What I thought about when we were solving this problem was...

22. I think a better approach to the task would have been...

23. The way I reached my conclusions was...

24. I would like to have more information about...

25. One idea I really liked was _____ because...

26. One idea I'd like to compliment a group member on is...

27. I can compare this information to...

28. Given this information, I predict...

29. I think this idea will work because...

30. If I were to change something, it would be _____ because...

The following list of behaviors can be used when observing the development of thinking strategies.

1. Contributing ideas.

2. Listening to the ideas of others.

3. Giving noncritical feedback.

4. Elaborating on ideas.

5. Verbally exploring the consequences of a decision before acting.

6. Examining the pros and cons of issues.

7. Summarizing ideas.

8. Sharing thoughts behind an idea or suggestion.

9. Taking time to think before attempting to solve a problem.

10. Developing and discussing a strategy before beginning work on a problem.

11. Asking others how they arrived at a decision or solution.

Reinforcing Internal Dialogue and Mediation: Alternative Solutions

GRADE LEVEL: 2 – Adult
GROUP SIZE: 3 – 4
GROUP ROLES: Recorder
MATERIALS: Paper and pencil
ACTIVITY:

Assign groups of 3 – 4 students each.

Write the following problem on the chalkboard (increase or decrease the difficulty to match the ability level of your students).

234

568

462

+ 128

Task: List as many ways as you can think of to arrive at a solution to this problem. Note: we are not looking for the correct answer but for methods to arrive at the answer.
Example: add the numbers from bottom to top.

Step 1:

Have each student work individually for three to four minutes. At the end of this time, students should tally the number of ways they have thought of.

Step 2:

Provide an equal amount of time for groups to combine their individual ideas into one list and generate additional ideas.

Step 3:

Discuss the activity with the class. Ask how many new ideas were generated when they worked together in their groups. Point out that when our minds are put together, we gain new ideas and learn from each other. Also point out, that during their group activity they were actually teaching each other new strategies for thinking. By sharing ideas, they have mediated each other's thinking processes; they have expanded their internal dialogue by gaining new ways to talk to themselves when approaching a problem.

Reinforcing the Concept of "Effective Thinker": Qualities

GRADE LEVEL: 1 – Adult

GROUP SIZE: 3 – 4

GROUP ROLES: Recorder

MATERIALS: Paper and pencil

ACTIVITY: Assign students to groups of three to four students each. Groups list as many qualities of a good thinker they can think of in five minutes. Each recorder shares his group's list information with the class. Write the lists on the chalkboard.

(Since younger students may not be able to write a list of responses, a group discussion followed by a sharing session may be substituted for written responses.)

Following the activity, discuss with the whole class the benefits of effective thinking strategies.

Writing Higher-Level Thinking Questions

GRADE LEVEL: 5 – adult

GROUP SIZE: 3 – 5

GROUP ROLES: Recorder

MATERIALS: Bloom's taxonomy (or whichever taxonomy you use); paper and pencil.

ACTIVITY:

Step 1:

Explain the differences among Bloom's six levels, providing examples for each category.

Step 2:

Give students a reading assignment.

Step 3:

Assign students to groups of three to five students each.

Step 4:

Groups write questions about the reading assignment for each of Bloom's six levels.

Step 5:
Groups each share and discuss their questions with the rest of the class.

NOTE: This activity could span two or more class sessions.

To Infuse higher level questions into lessons:

The following guide sheet will help you infuse higher level questioning into your lessons. Write the specific content of the lesson, then write an appropriate question for each thinking level related to that content.

Content: _____

QUESTIONS:

Knowledge (recall, identify, recognize, label):

Comprehension (translate, interpret, explain, describe, summarize, extrapolate):

Application (apply, solve, experiment, predict):

Analysis (connect, relate, classify, arrange, compare, infer):

Synthesis (produce, propose, design, plan, combine, formulate, compose, hypothesize):

Evaluation (appraise, judge, criticize, decide):

Enhancing Internal Dialogue: Why?

GRADE LEVEL: 3 – Adult

GROUP SIZE: 3 – 4

GROUP ROLES: Recorder

MATERIALS: Paper and pencil

ACTIVITY:

Assign students to groups of three or four students each.

Step 1:

Groups develop a list of reasons it's important to develop internal dialogue.

Step 2:

Groups then develop another list of reasons for why it's important to share their internal dialogue with others.

Step 3:

Each group recorder shares his group's lists with the rest of the class.

Step 4:

Whole class discusses ideas they gained from other groups.

Chapter 6

Wrapping Up

Michelle Beyers

A *Wrap Up* is a very brief activity which occurs immediately after each Simple Cooperation lesson (Simple Cooperation is a cooperative learning model designed by Jacqueline Rhoades and Margaret E. McCabe in 1984). Its primary purposes are to:

1. give each student the opportunity to think about his own cognitive and/or social behavior within a structure

2. provide the teacher with immediate feedback about the process each group or individual used to accomplish the task.

3. help measure the learning that has occurred.

4. reinforce a specific social skill, such as paraphrasing.

5. reinforce prior learning, new learning and/or the integration of prior and new learning.

Wrap-Up activities may be general or specific, related to the lesson's academic and/or social skills objective, written or verbal, and may be completed by individuals or small groups. Wrap-ups can also be completed in the large group setting.

The wrap-up activity may take as few as two or three minutes or it may take as many as twenty minutes to complete depending on the teacher's objective.

The following Wrap-Up activities reflect some of our personal favorites.

Small Group Discussion

GRADE LEVEL: Kindergarten – Adult
GROUP ROLES: Optional – Facilitator
TIME: 5 – 10 minutes
MATERIALS: None
ACTIVITY:

Each group discusses among themselves a specific such as:

- One way our group worked well together to accomplish the task was...

- I thought that the most interesting part of this assignment was...

- One way we can improve as a group is...

- How we're doing with...
  (praising, listening, claiming own thoughts, etc.)

- One way the content of this assignment relates to real life is...

- I liked this activity because...

- I didn't like this activity because...

and so on.

Students should be given a minute of "thinking time" before beginning group discussion. Allow about three minutes for group discussion, then, if time permits, ask each facilitator to share two or three of the group's responses with the whole class.

The Compliment

GRADE LEVEL: Kindergarten – Adult
ROLES: None
TIME: 5 – 10 minutes
MATERIALS: None
ACTIVITY:

1. Within the Simple Cooperation group, each member gives a compliment to the person on their right about how he has helped the group accomplish its task.

2. Compliments begin with one group member; for instance, the group member who is sitting closest to the wall clock, and then continues around the circle. Only one person speaks at a time. This allows each group member to hear all the compliments.

Feedback Cards

GRADE LEVEL: 1 – Adult
TIME: 3 – 5 minutes
MATERIALS: One 3 x 5 index card per student
ACTIVITY:

1. Feedback cards are used at the end of the group assignment and may be open-ended such as:

   a. Write your reaction to the lesson.

   b. Describe how you felt about this assignment.

   c. What was the best thing about this group activity.

   d. Write any concerns you have about this lesson.

   e. Write any questions you still have about the content of this lesson.

2. Feedback cards may be specific, such as:

   a. Rate your group on praising/sharing/asking questions/listening to others/or any other social skill you want to reinforce.

b. Write one new thing you learned about...(whatever the lesson content is).

c. How would you rate yourself on...(again, pick a social skill you've taught).

d. Write down the three most important facts in this lesson.

e. How can you use the information in this lesson outside this classroom.

f. How is (specific social skill) important in your life outside school.

Cards may be signed or left anonymous. You could collect and shuffle them and read them aloud to the class or use the information to adjust your next lesson.

The Wrap-Up Sheet

GRADE LEVEL: 2 – Adult
ROLES: None
TIME: 10 minutes
MATERIALS: Prepared Wrap-Up Sheet with one to five questions for each student.
ACTIVITY:

This is similar to the Feedback Cards except that the sheet with questions is prepared and distributed to students. Figure 18 demonstrates three of the many possible Wrap-Up sheets.

Questions must lend themselves to short responses.

1. Distribute prepared Wrap-Up Sheet to each student.

2. Allow two to five minutes for students to write their responses.

3. Teacher's option:

a. Students read their responses aloud.

b. Teacher collects responses and reads them aloud.

c. Teacher collects responses for personal review.

SAMPLE WRAP-UP FORMS

Sample #1

To me, the most important parts of this lesson were:

_____

_____

_____

_____

Sample #2

RATE YOURSELF—Circle the number that best describes how much YOU contributed to your group's assignment today.

LOW   HIGH

1   2   3   4   5   6   7   8   9   10

Sample #3

Complete the drawing that shows how you feel about today's group lesson.

The Fantasy

GRADE LEVEL: 2 – Adult
ROLES: None
TIME: 15 minutes
MATERIALS: Paper and pencil/pen
ACTIVITY:

1. Students are asked to use their imaginations and to create new ideas relevant to the topic they have just been working with.

   For example: if they had been studying a unit on famous inventors, they would be asked to pretend they are famous inventors themselves, and imagine a fantastic invention they would like to create.

2. Students are given a minute or two of "thinking time" before writing the name and description of their invention on paper.

3. Students then share their new inventions with their small group, or with the entire class, as time permits.

Chapter 7

Activities Across the Curriculum

Matt Johnston

This chapter offers twenty pages of academic activities and techniques that can be easily adapted to use with most subject areas and at most grade levels. There are several issues to consider before conducting an academic cooperative lesson:

1. Assign students to cooperative groups carefully. A heterogeneous grouping pattern gives students a greater opportunity to hear and discuss alternatives to approaching the assignment. Small cooperative groups reflect the class population in terms of performance, boy/girl and ethnic ratio.

2. Group size ranges from two to six students. Keep the groups small, say 3 – 4 students each until students have gained communication and problem solving skills and are experienced in participating in a cooperative group.

3. Academic objectives need to be appropriate for each member of the group.

4. Every cooperative lesson or activity includes a specific academic objective *and* a social skills objective, such as listening to each other. Students need to understand what the objectives of the activity are.

5. Allow students to learn and practice each social skill before integrating that skill into an academic activity.

6. Students need to sit together in such a way that they can hear and see each other.

7. Be sure students understand what they are to do, what group they're in, and where each group should gather to work together.

8. Assign group roles such as facilitator, recorder, praiser in each group as appropriate for the lesson and for the students' ability levels. Roles need to be taught, demonstrated or modeled and practiced.

9. Monitor each group's process by moving from group to group during the activity.

Cooperative Drawing

GRADE LEVEL: Preschool – 2

GROUP SIZE: 2

ROLES: None

MATERIALS: Construction or drawing paper, crayons or marking pens

ACTIVITY:

1. Group students in pairs. Each group decides on a subject for their drawing and tells teacher what they will draw.

2. Pairs work together for a specified amount of time to complete drawings.

3. Drawings are hung on bulletin board.

Matching

GRADE LEVEL: Preschool – 2

GROUP SIZE: 3

ROLES: None

MATERIALS: Two- or threepiece jigsaw puzzles

ACTIVITY:

1. Group students in pairs or triads and assign to workspace.

2. Each group receives the pieces needed to complete one puzzle per student.

3. The pieces are placed face-down in front of each group.

4. Students are given a specific amount of time, e.g., five or ten minutes, to turn the pieces face up and assemble the puzzles correctly.

Building the Alphabet

GRADE LEVEL: Preschool – 2

GROUP SIZE: 2 – 3

ROLES: Checker

MATERIALS: Alphabet tiles (or write the alphabet on construction paper squares)

ACTIVITY:

1. Assign students to groups of two or three.

2. Each group is given a complete set of "mixed-up" alphabet letters.

3. Students must arrange the letters in correct order from A to Z within a specified amount of time (five to ten minutes).

4. At the end of the allocated time, an answer sheet is given to the checker in each group and the group checks its answers for accuracy.

NOTE: Any sequencing task may use this same format.

Murals

(This activity can be used after a series of lessons on any subject that lends itself to visual representation, such as: farms; gardens; maps; inventions; botany; and so on.)

GRADE LEVEL: Preschool – 9

GROUP SIZE: 3 – 4

ROLES: None

MATERIALS: Varies, depending upon the type of mural the class is to make. Commonly used materials include: butcher paper; poster paint; marking pens; paste; scissors; sample pictures or stencils of objects to be put on mural.

ACTIVITY:

1. Assign students to homogeneous groups of 3 – 4.

2. Each group is given the assignment to complete one section of the mural. For instance, if the assignment is to make a mural of a farm, one group would complete the background, including the sky, grass, dirt, and trees; another group would make the chickens; another group, the cows; another, the buildings, if any; and so on.

3. Students need to receive instructions about the relative size of the objects to be included on the mural.

4. After each group has completed the assignment, the teacher assists the class (as necessary) in attaching all the component parts to the background.

Group Worksheet

GRADE LEVEL: 1 – Adult
GROUP SIZE: 3 – 5
ROLES: Facilitator, Recorder, Timekeeper
MATERIALS: Worksheets
ACTIVITY:

1. Assign students to groups of 3 – 5 members each, depending on grade level and lesson objective.

2. Assign a Facilitator, Recorder, and Timekeeper for each group.

3. Distribute worksheets to each student. It is important that each student in a group has the same worksheet, though worksheets may differ between groups.

4. Provide one group answer sheet to each group.

5. Students first work individually on their own worksheets for a specified amount of time.

6. Group members discuss each question one at a time, sharing their individual answers and how they arrived at them. The Facilitator makes certain that each group member has the opportunity to share responses.

7. Group members determine the correct response which the Recorder writes on the clean answer sheet. It's important for the Recorder to read back the response for each question to verify accuracy.

8. Each group member signs the answer sheet to indicate agreement with the responses. The Facilitator then hands in the group's work to the teacher.

Where's the Beginning?

GRADE LEVEL: 3 – 12
GROUP SIZE: 3 – 4
ROLES: Recorder and Reader
TIME: 15 – 30 minutes
MATERIALS: Paper, pencil, short story
PREPARATION: Teacher selects a short story or report with a strong and interesting ending. Duplicate only the ending of the story or report for each group for this activity.

ACTIVITY:

1. Assign students to groups.

2. Appoint the Recorder and Reader for each group.

3. Distribute one copy of the duplicated ending to each group.

4. Reader reads the ending aloud to the group.

5. Group discusses the part of the story or report they have and write the story's or report's beginning.

6. Recorder writes group's response.

7. Recorder reads group's completed story AND/OR teacher collects completed stories and posts them on the wall where everyone can read them.

Study Groups

GRADE LEVEL: 2 – Adult

GROUP SIZE: 3 – 5

ROLES: Checker, test-taker, challenger

MATERIALS: 20 index cards, numbered 1 – 20; a list of 20 questions with answers. These should be short answer questions with a definite right answer.

ACTIVITY:

1. Assign students to groups of three to five, depending on grade level and social skills ability. Groups may be homogeneous or heterogeneous, depending on the lesson objective.

2. Three roles are assigned in each group: Checker; Test-Taker; Challenger. These roles are rotated in a clockwise direction after each question.

3. A specific amount of time is allocated for the study session (10 – 20 minutes works well).

4. The index cards are shuffled and placed in a stack face down in the center of the table.

5. The Test-Taker draws a card, states the number, and places it face up on the table.

6. The Checker locates the corresponding number on the question/answer sheet and reads the question.

7. The Test-Taker responds.

8. The Checker asks if there are any challenges. This is asked whether the Test-Taker gave a correct or incorrect response.

9. If there are any challenges, the Challenger sitting closest to the Test-Taker's right side may provide an answer.

10. The Checker then states the correct answer. The person who gave the correct response, the Test-Taker or the Challenger, keeps the numbered index card.

11. If neither the Test-Taker nor the Challenger were correct, the index card is placed at the bottom of the stack.

12. Roles are then rotated one person to the right (clockwise). Study continues until the end of the time.

HINTS:

1. Study questions and answers must be clear and concise. There must be a very definite "right" answer. Spelling, vocabulary, math facts and other knowledge level questions are most suited for this activity.

2. To avoid confusion, require students to give the precise answer that is on the answer sheet.

3. When first initiating this activity, write the group roles on index cards. The cards can be rotated clockwise after each question. This helps students remember what role they are.

VARIATION:

Include a penalty for incorrect challenges. This helps deter students who simply like to challenge others. When challengers are incorrect, they must place a previously won card back in the stack. This means that a student may not challenge until he or she has "won" a card.

Writing Assignments

GRADE LEVEL: 2 – Adult
GROUP SIZE: 2 – 3
ROLES: Recorder; Optional: Facilitator and/or Timekeeper
TIME: 30 – 45 minutes
MATERIALS: Paper and pencils
ACTIVITY:

1. Assign students to groups of 2 –3.

2. Assign a topic on which they are to write.

3. Groups should each discuss the assigned topic and decide what they will include in their group paper. Brainstorming may be a useful techniques for the groups to use. A facilitator and timekeeper would be appropriate for the problem solving part of this assignment.

4. Discussion about what to include in the paper should only last five to fifteen minutes.

5. Each group should decide how they will approach the writing assignment. Will each person complete a sentence, paragraph, section? Will they work together to write each sentence?

6. No matter what approach the group uses, the recorder will write the final product on one sheet of paper.

7. The actual time for writing the paper will be 15 – 30 minutes.

8. Each group reviews its paper and makes any desired changes or necessary corrections.

9. Each group member signs the finished paper to indicate agreement with the finished product.

10. Paper is handed in to teacher and/or read to class.

Cooperative Group Exam/Quiz

(Takes longer but students learn a lot more.)

NOTE: We do not promote graded group exams in grades K – 12; use scores as self-evaluation or as bonus points. We do use cooperative group exams in adult and college classes, however.

GRADE LEVEL: 2 – Adult
GROUP SIZE: 2 – 5
ROLES: Facilitator, Time-Keeper and Recorder
TIME: Depends on the test; plan a 15-minute test.
MATERIALS: Short group exam/quiz, text book and/or other appropriate information; paper and pencils

ACTIVITY:

This is an open-book exam/quiz and may be used as a study session, or you can give your students bonus points for their performance. It would be appropriate to follow up with an individual assessment to evaluate mastery of the content material.

Exam/Quiz should be short and simple, especially the first few times students are asked to participate in a cooperative group testing situation.

1. Assign students to heterogeneous or homogeneous groups of 2 – 5 students each, depending upon your objectives, the content of the test, and the structure in which your students have been working.

2. Distribute a copy of the test to each student.

3. Each group discusses each question and decides what the correct response is. The group Facilitator will help keep the group on task and will also help the group reach a consensus decision for each question.

4. The group's recorder writes the response on a clean copy of the test.

5. The Timekeeper should give the group half-time, ten and five minute warnings.

6. The recorder will read the responses a final time to be sure its been written as the group intended.

7. All group members sign the test to indicate agreement with the responses.

8. Tests are submitted to you for grading.

Group Research Projects and Reports

GRADE LEVEL: 3 – Adult

GROUP SIZE: 3 – 5

ROLES: Facilitator and Recorder

MATERIALS: Group assignment sheet, reference materials, paper and pencils

PREPARATION: Each student is given an assignment appropriate to his ability level; this requires the teacher to predetermine different assignments.

GRADING: A single group grade or bonus points.

ACTIVITY:

1. Assign students to heterogeneous groups of 3 – 5 members each.

2. Assign a Facilitator and Recorder for each group.

3. Sample schedule for multi-day assignment:

   Day 1: Facilitator reviews assignment with the group to ensure understanding. Each member should be aware of his or her own part in the complete project, the components of the assignment as well as the content and location of various reference materials.

   Days 2 & 3: Team members work independently on their respective assignments, gathering information, taking notes and constructing outlines for their own sections.

   Day 4: Team members meet and discuss what they have each learned; each member gives a progress report.

   Day 5: The group report is written following the teacher's guidelines. The Facilitator keeps the discussion "on track" and moving; the Recorder writes the report. When the report is completed, the Recorder will need to read it aloud to the group to verify the content is as the group wants it.

   All group members sign the report to indicate their agreement with the finished product.

The group project/report is an ideal way to use the strengths of each group member because each student is assigned a part of the task appropriate to skill and ability level; reference materials at the student's reading and comprehension levels are also provided

Example:

The research project focusing on the Westward Movement is assigned. One group member might be assigned to research famous scouts and to make a list of names and their famous deeds. Another member might analyze the economic impact of the Westward Movement on the country. A third student might research the impact of of this movement on the Native American Indian population. One student might even build a model of a conestoga wagon or draw a scene the people might have seen at that time.

Each and every student makes an important contribution to the project.

Forming an Opinion

GRADE LEVEL: 4 – Adult
GROUP SIZE: 3 – 5
ROLES: Facilitator, Recorder, Timekeeper
TIME: 1 – 2 hours
MATERIALS: Information sheets, film (or lecture) about controversial issue relevant to the curriculum or a current event

ACTIVITY:

1. Form heterogeneous groups of 3 – 5 students each; assign a Facilitator, Recorder and Timekeeper for each group.

2. Show film or give lecture.

3. Groups have 10 – 20 minutes to discuss pros and cons of the issue. Recorder writes the major points of discussion, noting pros in one column and cons in another column. Facilitator assures each group member has opportunity to state thoughts and opinions.

4. Another 10 – 20 minutes are provided for students to reach a consensus decision on where their group "stands" on the issue. (It may be helpful to review the problem solving/decision making processes described earlier.)

5. At the end of the time period, the Facilitator of each group reports the group's decision and rationale behind their decision.

If the group has been unable to arrive at a consensus decision, the Facilitator shares that fact and discusses the problems they encountered in their decision-making process.

The Great Debate

GRADE LEVEL: 4 – Adult
GROUP SIZE: one-half the class
ROLES: Facilitator and Recorder (Optional: Timekeeper)
TIME: 35 – 50 Minutes
MATERIALS: Information sheets, film or lecture on controversial issue

ACTIVITY:

1. Divide the class in half, forming two debate teams. Each team is assigned a position they will take regarding the issue. For example: providing classes in school about drugs and their effects. One team would support providing such classes regardless of the individual team members' own opinions; the other team would debate against providing such instruction in schools.

2. Assign a Facilitator and Recorder for each team. A Timekeeper may also be assigned for each team or the teacher may act as Timekeeper.

Steps:

a. Show the film or deliver an orientation lecture about the issue.

b. Allow 20 – 30 minutes following the film/lecture for the teams to discuss the critical factors involved in their assigned positions and how they will support that position.

The team's Recorder writes the key points on the chalk-board, chart paper, or notepaper.

c. Place two chairs facing each other at the front of the room (or in the middle, whichever works best for your classroom setting). All other chairs are placed on the sides of the room.

d. Team members sit together. Teams face each other.

e. The Great Debate begins!

15 to 20 minutes are allowed for the debate. The rules are:

a. To speak, a team member must sit in the chair.

b. Teams alternate speakers with each speaker limited to one (1) minute. The teacher may choose to be the Timekeeper OR assign a student to be Timekeeper before assigning teams.

c. Each team member must speak during the debate.

d. A team member may speak more than one time but only for one minute at a time.

e. There must always be a team member in each debate chair.

f. To get into the debate chair, the team member must walk up to the person sitting in the chair and tap him on his shoulder. The present speaker may continue speaking for the rest of his minute, if he wants, then moves out of the chair to allow the other team member to be seated.

g. If more than one team member wants to take the debate chair at the same time, the team Facilitator establishes a waiting line.

h. It is part of the Facilitator's job to make sure each team member sits in the debate chair and contributes at least once during the debate.

Following The Great Debate, the Wrap-Up will be a general discussion about the strongest points presented on each side.

Recall Matrix

GRADE LEVEL: 4 – Adult
GROUP SIZE: 2 – 4
ROLE: Recorder
TIME: 20 minutes
MATERIALS: Recall matrix and pencil
PURPOSE: Reinforce previously taught skills
PREPARATION:

1. Design two-dimensional matrix with categories listed vertically and characteristics horizontally. Example: How to change nouns from singular to plural.

   Categories = nouns, e.g.,. "candy" "bird" "sheep"

   Characteristics = drop "y" add "ies"; add "s"; leave as is (plural is same as singular form.)

	Drop "y": Add "ies"	Add "s"	Leave as is – same singular or plural
Candy			
Bird			
Sheep			

ACTIVITY:

1. Form groups of two to four students.

2. Distribute one matrix form to each student.

3. Students reach consensus decision for each answer.

4. Recorder writes group's answer on matrix. Example: "Candies" would be written in the blank cell under the heading "Drop 'y'; add 'ies'."

5. Students sign answer matrix form to indicate agreement with responses.

VARIATION: Students put check mark in appropriate cell instead of writing response.

(Adapted from P.M. Cunningham and J.W. Cunningham, Feb. 1987. Content area reading-writing lessons. *The Reading Teacher*, 40, 506 – 512.)

Find the Quality

GRADE LEVEL: 2 – Adult

GROUP SIZE: 2 – 4

TIME: 15 – 20 minutes

ROLE(S): Recorder; When appropriate, i.e. with reading passages, the role of Reader will be useful.

MATERIALS: Reading passage, short story, art picture, music selection

Example:

Using a musical selection students are studying, such as "Peter and the Wolf," form matrices listing various instruments such as the violin, bassoon, piano, etc. on the vertical axis with plus (+) and minus (–) on the horizontal axis. Students would listen to the music selection and make a checkmark under the appropriate column based on whether or not they hear that musical instrument.

ACTIVITY:

1. Form groups of two to four students.

2. Distribute one matrix form to each student.

3. Students reach consensus decision for each answer.

4. Recorder checks the appropriate column.

5. Students sign answer matrix form to indicate agreement with responses.

Instruments	+	−
Piano		
Violin		
Bassoon		
Viola		
Flute		
Oboe		
French Horn		

(Adapted from P.M. Cunningham and J.W. Cunningham, Feb. 1987. Content area reading-writing lessons. *The Reading Teacher*, 40, 506 – 512.)

Application Analysis

GRADE LEVELs: 4 – Adult
GROUP SIZE: 3 – 4
TIME: 15 – 20 minutes
ROLE(S): Recorder; Reader
MATERIALS: Reading passage & application analysis form
ACTIVITY:

1. Assign students to groups of 3 – 4 members.

2. Assign a chapter or part of a chapter or story to the class as a reading assignment. The actual reading can be completed in class or as homework depending on the length.

3. Give each group an "Application Analysis Form."

4. After reading the selection, students complete the Application Analysis Form. This form requires students to first analyze the information they have read in each paragraph and then to determine how the reading can be applied in their present or near future life. Students analyze one paragraph at a time.

5. At the end of the time limit, each group shares their results with the entire class.

Example:

The following is an example of how to use Application Analysis. We're using paragraphs from the Communication Chapter in *The Nurturing Classroom*.

"Check Out Perceptions"

A third clarifying technique is to "check out" your perceptions. Checking your perceptions means that the listener looks beyond the words and attempts to understand how the speaker is really feeling. This is important when the listener is unsure of the speaker's feelings.

Checking your perceptions is also important when the listener thinks she is getting a double message; that is, when the words say one thing and the nonverbal message says something else. Perception-checking helps the listener understand the "true" message the speaker is trying to convey."

Paragraph Number	Summary of information	Application, i.e., how to use the information
Paragraph #1	Using perception checking to understand speaker's feelings.	When I talk with anyone, I can use perception checking to avoid confusion and misunderstandings
Paragraph #2	Use perception checking when verbal and nonverbal messages don't seem to agree with each other	I can use perception checking when I don't understand what my friends are saying.

(Adapted from: K. Patricia Cross and Thomas A. Angelo *Classroom Assessment Techniques*)

Building a Story

GRADE LEVEL: 1 – Adult

GROUP SIZE: 2 – 4

ROLE: Recorder — This recorder will not write anything; he or she will arrange the paragraphs in the sequence the group determines.

TIME: 10 – 30 minutes

MATERIALS: A one to three page story cut up into paragraphs.

PREPARATION: Select a one to three page story, as appropriate for grade and ability level. Cut the story up by paragraphs. Mix the paragraphs up so the story is out of sequence. Put the paragraphs in a packet; they could be paper clipped together, put in an envelope, or put in a manila folder. The teacher will need one packet for each group. The stories do not have to be the same for each group, i.e. each group could have a different story.

ACTIVITY:

1. Assign students to groups of 2 – 4.

2. Give one story packet to each group.

3. Group members read the paragraphs and decide how to sequence the paragraphs so the story makes sense.

4. The "Recorder" places the paragraphs in the agreed-upon sequence. (It would be a good idea if the recorder numbered the paragraphs sequentially or glued them in place on other sheets of paper.)

5. Each group reads their story to the class.

NOTE: It is probable that groups will sequence the paragraphs differently than the original story and that the new story will make sense.

Justice

GRADE LEVEL:	4 – 12
GROUP SIZE:	3 – 4
ROLE(S):	Recorder and Spokesperson
TIME:	10 – 30 minutes
MATERIALS:	Paper and pencil/pen
PREPARATION:	Teacher leads a class discussion on justice, e.g., what does "justice" mean, how can you tell "justice" has been achieved.

ACTIVITY:

1. Assign students in groups of 3 – 4.

2. Assign student to write a code of justice by which they think everyone can live.

3. Group members sign answer sheet to indicate agreement with response.

4. Spokesperson from each group reads the group's "Code of Justice."

FOLLOW-UP: The other groups react to each "Code of Justice," i.e., they discuss which parts would be acceptable to them and which wouldn't and why. Work towards a class consensus on a "Code of Justice."

117

The U.S.A.

GRADE LEVEL: 4 – 12
GROUP SIZE: 3 – 4
ROLE: Recorder and Spokesperson
TIME: 20 – 30 minutes
MATERIALS: Paper and pencil/pen
PREPARATION: Discuss the geographical boundaries of the U.S.A. Talk about how the U.S.A. is a concept as well as a geographical location. (This is true of most, if not all, countries so follow-up activities can focus on other countries.)

ACTIVITY:

1. Assign students to groups of 3 – 4 members.

2. Appoint the Recorder and Spokesperson for each group.

3. Each group writes on paragraph on "what the U.S.A. means to *me*."

4. Spokespersons share their groups' responses.

5. Discuss the similarities and differences between and among group responses.

Where's the Answer

GRADE LEVEL: 3 – Adult
GROUP SIZE: 2 – 4
ROLE: Recorder and Reader
TIME: 20 – 30 minutes
MATERIALS: Teacher-made list of questions relevant to specific content area being studied

ACTIVITY:

1. Assign students to groups of 2 – 4.

2. Distribute prepared questions.

3. Students read questions and list as many sources they can think of for obtaining the answers.

4. Students sign answer sheet to indicate agreement with group responses and turn list in to teacher.

FOLLOW UP: Assign each group two or three questions to research using the sources they listed. Groups each write a short report on the questions and answers they discovered.

History Mapping

GRADE LEVEL: 1 – Adult
GROUP SIZE: 3 – 4
ROLE: Recorder
TIME: 15 – 30 minutes
MATERIALS: Paper and Pencil/Pen
PREPARATION: Select a topic relevant to current curriculum such as:

1. What we have studied in Science, History, Literature, etc.

2. Specific topics such as: Major Battles of the Civil War; Presidents of the United States; Scientific Discoveries related to Antibiotics.

ACTIVITY:

1. Assign students to groups of 3 – 4.

2. Instruct students to develop a map of activities placed in historical (chronological) sequence.

3. Group members agree on sequence.

4. Recorder draws the group's historical map (see next page).

5. Each group member signs the final map to indicate agreement with the group's response.

Example:

It Takes Lots of Words to Make a Picture

GRADE LEVEL: 2 -12

GROUP SIZE: 2 – 3

ROLES: Recorder

TIME: 15 – 20 minutes

MATERIALS: Paper, pencil, selected object

PREPARATION: Teacher selects objects such as vase, pencil, shoe box, comb, etc.

ACTIVITY:

1. Assign students to groups of 2 – 3.

2. Appoint a Recorder for each group.

3. Give each group a different object.

4. Have groups "paint" a verbal picture of the object by describing it in full detail. (Optional: You may provide a measuring tape or ruler if you would like greater precision in the description.)

5. Recorder writes group's description and students sign response page to indicate agreement.

6. Teacher collects papers.

7. Place all objects in full view of class.

8. Teacher reads descriptions and class guesses which object is being described.

WRAP-UP ACTIVITY:

Class discusses what was included in the descriptions that were easy to guess.

Chapter 8

Breaking Up

Helen Hayes

Each group eventually reaches the time when they must "break up." The group time ends. In this case, the school term ends; students will move on to the next grade level and to other classrooms.

This can be a very hard time for students in a Simple Cooperation classroom. Students are likely to experience sadness and anxiety when it comes time for the group to disband and the more cohesive and cooperative the class is, the more difficult it is for them to leave the group. Students experience a mini-grief cycle, a time when they don't know exactly why they're having unpleasant feelings.

This is a time when conflict is likely to erupt in your classroom. Students first entered your class not knowing exactly what to expect: Would anyone like them? Would they have any friends? Would they get along with the teacher? Would they be able to do the assigned work? Since that first day, they have become members of a cohesive group, a group that is built on mutual trust, respect, and caring. Now they must leave the safety and support of this group. That is anxiety-provoking for any age.

You can help your students work through their feelings of impending loss and anxiety by carefully planning activities for the end of the term. The activities must be such that they help you and your students immortalize the group, things that provide a "living" memory and that also redirect your students' energies to the next phase in their lives.

The following Breaking-Up activities will help your students bring the necessary closure to your class as a group.

Remember Forever

GRADE LEVEL: 3 – 8

GROUP SIZE: 2 – 3

ROLE: Recorder and Spokesperson

TIME: 10 – 15 minutes

MATERIALS: Paper and pencil/pen

PREPARATION: About six to eight weeks before the end of the school year, the teacher leads a class discussion on special moments in a person's life.

ACTIVITY:

1. Assign students to groups of 2 – 3 members

2. Each group decides on one moment in their classroom experience so far this year that they would like to remember forever.

3. Groups then brainstorm ideas about what they could do to remember that moment.

4. Group Spokespersons share responses with rest of class.

The following list of activities can be used in most grade levels to help students leave this group.

Sharing Individual Pictures

Students may bring photos to class or use an instant picture camera to take candid shots at school. The pictures can be placed on a bulletin board before students take them home.

Cooperative Group Pictures

Pictures of each cooperative group working together can be taken throughout the year with prints made for each group member. A copy of each picture can be put on a bulletin board until the end of the year. This reminds students of how many groups they participated in successfully.

Sharing Class Pictures

Take a picture of the entire class involved in an activity, duplicate and distribute to each student. (Of course, the class picture taken by the school photographer can be used but it isn't quite as much fun.)

Copies of Special Small Group Projects

Cooperative groups can reproduce a project that was special to the group. Each group member then keeps a copy of the project as a memento. (Examples: term papers; research papers; essays; literature critiques; an especially difficult test; any type of report; etc.)

Autograph Books

These can be made by students so that each page has a statement or picture that is meaningful to students. They can be bound into a "book" in many ways: stitching; velobind; spiral bind; stapled; glued.

Journals or Scrapbooks

As a final project, students could write a journal or make a scrapbook, noting special events and other memories. A journal or scrapbook could also be kept during the year with entries made periodically. This really helps students remember how they felt about the various activities.

Class Story

At the end of the year students write a story about their class. This is a great creative writing assignment. The story would be duplicated for each student to take home. If the story were completed early enough, excerpts of it could be printed in the school newspaper or bulletin.

Sharing Feelings

This can be done in small groups with each group writing their thoughts and feelings, then sharing their comments with the rest of the class. Another alternative is to have individuals share their feelings and thoughts with the entire class by conducting a whip. OR the entire class can brainstorm their feelings and achievements.

Visiting Classrooms

Very often, elementary students visit the junior high school and graduating junior high students visit the high school. But elementary students do not usually have the opportunity to visit the next grade level classroom. Even if a school has five classes of the next grade level, a brief visit (5 minutes) to each one would help alleviate some anxiety about their forthcoming move.

Orientation Sessions

If visiting the next grade level is impossible, the next best thing is to have those teachers visit the present classroom and briefly explain what can be expected in that grade level.

Sharing Future Goals

Students get together in small groups and discuss what they would like to be when they grow up. Groups brainstorm about what they think each one will need to learn in order to fulfill their goals.

Beautification

Plant trees or bushes on campus grounds with a sign "From the class of...."

Art Projects

An art project such as painting a mural for the classroom or for the school, making a sculpture, stained glass designs that can be hung by the window, macramé plant holders, drawings, picture collage, etc. The mural can be painted on canvas, plywood or cardboard and attached to a wall or it can be painted directly on a wall.

Giving Imaginary Gifts

Students' names are placed in a container. Each student draws a name and decides what he or she would most like to give to his recipient. Students then sit in a circle and each student "gives" his gift by describing what it is, walking to the student and placing the imaginary gift in his or her hands. Gifts can be intangibles such as happiness or fun for the summer or they can be tangible items such as a new bike or whatever.

Leaving a Gift

This is similar to the individual imaginary gift. The class (or small groups) decide, if it were possible, what they would most like to give the world. Responses usually include such things as peace, food for everyone, clear communication, happiness.

Artifacts

Students place different artifacts in a container with a note and bury it someplace on campus with the idea it will be found by later generations.

Letters

Students, in small groups or in one large group, write a letter to: the students who will follow them in this class; the principal; their parents; the teacher; each other.

Class Yearbook

Each page is devoted to one or two students. A picture of the student is placed at the top with information about the student, such as: birthday; where born; how long in school; brothers and sisters; the funniest/most interesting thing that happened to the student that year; accomplishments and achievements; and whatever else the students might want to immortalize. These books can be made easily with a computer and "desk-top" publishing or word processing programs. They can be stapled or bound in some other way.

Chapter 9

Jigsaw Variations

Amber Lemon

The Jigsaw technique is one of the most powerful methods to use when teaching and studying narrative material such as literature, specific aspects of science, social studies, social sciences, and related areas where concepts rather than specific skills are the objective. Jigsaw may also be used successfully for art and problem solving activities. By using the Jigsaw approach, the teacher can cover large amounts of material in less time with greater learning and retention.

The first published jigsaw process (1978) was developed by Elliot Aronson and colleagues at the University of Texas.

In 1980, Dr. Robert Slavin and his colleagues at The Johns Hopkins University, modified Aronson's Jigsaw.

Without a doubt, teachers have been using different forms of the "Jigsaw" approach for many years. For example, as early as 1974 one of the present authors was using forms of this approach and simply calling it group collaboration; in other words, "survival" — a way to get more information to college students and workshop participants in less time with less work and time on the student's part.

College students historically have initiated study teams, breaking up the reading assignments among group members, having each synopse parts of the texts, then sharing the information and studying together. We should, however, be grateful to both Dr. Aronson and Dr. Slavin for formalizing the process and providing a database demonstrating the Jigsaw's validity as a learning technique.

Careful attention to certain logistics will enhance the jigsaw experience for your students:

1. Goal or Objective

Informing students of the expected outcome (goal or objective) of the jigsaw activity will enhance their learning experience. State your objective clearly; in fact, write it on the board and briefly discuss it with your class.

2. Materials

Each jigsaw team needs materials; the type of materials depends on the jigsaw model you are using and the lesson you are teaching. Whatever materials are used, it's important to continually convey the message that teams are exactly that – TEAMS – and their members must help each other learn the content. Materials needed will be discussed within each model of Jigsaw.

3. Group Size

Three to six members in the group is best. And remember, the less skilled students are in communication and problem solving skills, the smaller the group should be.

4. Group Membership

Heterogeneous groups almost always work and this type of grouping gives students more opportunity to increase thinking paths, thus enhancing higher level thinking skills.

5. Group Roles

Assign group roles as appropriate for the lesson. Remind students they are always "group members."

6. Group Member Seating Arrangement

Group members should sit close enough to see and hear each other but not so close as to threaten "personal space" or "territory."

7. Room & Furniture Arrangement

Since teachers rarely have the luxury of selecting their own furniture, you must make what you have work — students can sit on the floor, on counter tops, on chairs in small circles, clustered at the end of a rectangular table, at round tables, at movable desks turned so that four desks are clustered together or in any other arrangement that allows for small group cooperative activities.

8. Required Time

The amount of time required to complete a jigsaw is also dependent upon the type of jigsaw and the lesson content. This will also be discussed within the description of each Jigsaw model.

Jigsaw emphasizes team building activities before and during the activity. As stated at the beginning, it is also one of the most useful approaches to cover massive amounts of material in the shortest possible time because the content to be learned is divided into sections. Students read individual sections which may be entirely different from the parts read by their team-mates. Thus, each team member becomes valuable to the team as a whole. Students develop a sense of responsibility for their own learning as well as that of their team-mates.

JIGSAW I

(The original Jigsaw was developed by Elliot Aronson, a professor at the University of Santa Cruz. Reference: Aronson, Elliot, et al. *The Jigsaw Classroom.* Beverly Hills: Sage Publications, 1978. What follows is a slightly modified version of the original Jigsaw.)

Students are assigned to two groups: a "home" team and an "expert" team. The home team is usually a heterogeneous grouping of 3 – 6 students. Each member of the home team is assigned a specific part of the material to learn. In other words, the entire material is divided into the same number of sections as there are members in the team. (Each section must make sense in and of itself. Depending upon the material, we often find it helpful to provide an introduction or overview of the content which all students read prior to reading their assigned section.) Each home team then has a member responsible for a specific section of the material. After reading their respective sections individually, each home-team member meets with his counterparts from the other teams; this forms the "expert" group. "Expert" groups study their material and together decide how best to teach this to the other members of their "home" team. When each home team member shares his or her information, the group members will have all the information they need to pass the subsequent test.

For example: if you were studying a unit on any foreign country, one member of the team might read a study sheet or chapter about its industry, another about its climate, another member could study the general politics of the country, another could study its geography, and so on. Each home-team member would be assigned a number which would correspond to the section he or she was responsible for learning. (For example: #1s = industry; #2s = climate; #3s = politics; #4s = geography.)

MATERIALS:

You can develop your own materials assuring that each section is at the appropriate ability level for students (example...if the #1s were high performing readers, #2 and #3 average performers and the #4s were low performing readers, you would design the reading assignments at each student's reading ability level; the section for #1s could be more difficult OR it could be greater in quantity than that for the #4s).

TIME REQUIRED:

You will have to determine three different amounts of time:

1. the amount of time needed to read the assigned material in home groups

2. the amount of time the "expert" groups will have to study their sections and determine how to teach their home team members

3. the amount of time each student will have to share their part of the information

The allocated times will vary based on your students' age level and the complexity of the material. On an average, allow about three minutes per page to read, two to three minutes per page to study in the expert groups and one and a half minutes to two minutes per page to share the information. Always allow just a little less time than your students think they need; this helps students learn to synthesize and keeps them on task.

SEQUENCE:

1. Assign home teams and tell them where in the classroom they should sit together.

2. Distribute individual sections of the material to students within home teams.

3. Students read their section.

4. Assign expert teams to specific locations in the room.

5. Expert teams discuss, study and determine how best to teach their material to the rest of their home team members.

6. Experts return to their home team and teach their section to the other members.

7. General class discussion of the entire material.

SAMPLE SCHEDULE:

Day 1.

Assign home teams and distribute reading material. Students read their sections.

Day 2.

Expert teams meet to discuss and study their sections.

Day 3.

Expert team members return to their home group and teach their unique material to the other members.

General class discussion of all material and/or quiz to determine learning.

SOME VARIATIONS WE USE:

1. Have students read material at home.

2. Instead of preparing reading material, assign chapters or parts of chapters to each member.

3. Give each expert team a specific topic and have them research that area in the library.

4. Use Jigsaw for group writing projects with each member responsible for a specific section of the essay.

5. Jigsaw can also be used for other types of activities such as designing and constructing/painting/drawing murals, collages, other art projects; spelling or vocabulary words; math facts.

JIGSAW II

(Developed by Robert Slavin at The Johns Hopkins University. Reference: Slavin, Robert E. *Using Student Team Learning: The Johns Hopkins Team Learning Project*. Maryland, The Johns Hopkins University, 1980. What follows is a slightly modified version of Slavin's model.)

Jigsaw II, like the original Jigsaw by Aronson, can be used whenever the material to be studied is written in narrative form. It is most beneficial for subjects such as social studies, literature, parts of science and related areas in which the concepts rather than skills are the learning goals.

The basic material for Jigsaw II can be a chapter, story, biography or any other narrative material.

Again, as in the original Jigsaw, students are assigned to two groups: a "home" team and an "expert" team. The home team is usually a heterogeneous grouping of 3 – 6 students. Students all read the same material. However, each member of the "home-team" is given an "Expert Worksheet" which lists specific topics, aspects, or questions for the student to focus on during the reading. After reading the chapter, section, story, etc., students get together with their counterparts from the other "home-teams," study their specific assignments and decide how best to share/teach their topics to the rest of their home-team members. After the allotted time (depending on the material, this might be anywhere between 15 minutes and several class sessions), "Experts" return to their original home-teams and share/teach their information with the rest of their team.

For example: If a story were read, one member of each home team might focus on how the main theme is developed throughout the story, another might focus on the development of the main characters, another on what part the minor characters play in the sequence, etc.

STEPS:

1. Decide what material will be used for the Jigsaw. The quantity can be as much as the teacher would cover in 2 – 3 days.

2. Select four or five themes or topics that are central to the reading material.

3. Develop "Expert Worksheets" for each topic or theme. The worksheet will tell students exactly what they should focus on while they are reading the material. The selected themes should recur during the reading rather than be something that is mentioned only once.

4. Determine the student group assignments...these should be as heterogeneous groups of four to five students each and should represent a cross-section of your class.

5. Determine the "expert" group assignments; these may be more homogeneous. Again, rank your students from high to low relative to performance in this subject area in your class.

6. Introduce Jigsaw II to your students. Example: "For the next several weeks we are going to be using a new way of learning. It's called Jigsaw II. In Jigsaw II, you will be working in teams; in fact, you'll be working in two teams: your home team and an "expert" team — it's called "expert" because you will study specific material together and will become an "expert" in that specific material — then, you'll return to your home team and teach that material to the rest of your team members.

7. Tell students which home team they'll be on and designate a spot for them to sit together. They can then select a name for their team.

8. Distribute the reading material. Tell students: "The first step in this process is to read the "expert worksheet" I'm about to give you, then read the material looking for the information identified on your "expert worksheet."

9. When all students have finished reading, introduce the "expert" groups. Designate the area where each group should convene. Explain they should now discuss the information and decide how to best share/teach it to their other group members.

10. Following this study session (which could last from 15 minutes to two or three class sessions depending upon the material), the "experts" return to their home teams and take turns sharing/teaching their specific topics.

11. Following the sharing, hold a general class discussion and/or give a quiz.

SEQUENCE:

1. Assign home teams and distribute reading material. (10 min.)

2. Distribute Expert Worksheets and assign topics. (5 min.)

3. Students read material. (Time varies.)

4. Students meet in "expert" groups. (Usually about 30 minutes but can range between 15 minutes and two or three sessions.)

5. Students return and teach their info to rest of home group. (Usually about 10 minutes per topic area but ranges between 5 minutes and longer.)

6. Discussion and/or quiz.

NOTE: We've often found it more efficient to have students read the material at home as part of their homework assignment.

Jigsaw III

(Developed by Jacqueline Rhoades &
Margaret E. McCabe, 1974).

The modified Jigsaw is very similar to Aronson's original Jigsaw. The difference is that only expert groups are formed. Each expert group studies the material and then teaches that material to the rest of the class as a whole.

The modified Jigsaw is very useful for all narrative-type material as well as for any problem or question that has more than one right answer. For example, a problem may be presented to the class such as: "After reading the events surrounding the Boston Tea Party determine how else the citizens might have resolved their problems" or "After reading Chapter 10 in the Science text (or the Algebra or Geometry text) determine what mnemonic devices you can use to remember the formulas" (each team could actually be responsible for certain formulas and teach those to the entire class) or "What do you think the three most significant results of [some current news story] will be?" You can even use this process for math problems, each group working on specific problems, then sharing the problem, the answer and the process for reaching that answer with the rest of the class.

This model, like the original Jigsaw, emphasizes group cooperation and social skill development.

Homogeneous or heterogeneous groups may be formed dependent upon the topic to be discussed. As always, groups of 3 – 6 members would be assigned.

STEPS:

1. Determine the assignment and its objective.

2. Assign students to groups.

3. Tell groups where to convene.

4. Allow groups to choose a group name.

5. Assign group roles as appropriate to the lesson.

6. Give a mini-lecture about the material.

7. Give students their assignments (having them read the assignment as homework often works well).

8. Provide class time for students to study their part of the assignment and prepare to teach it to the rest of the class.

9. Student teams present to class.

10. Class discussion or individual quiz to check mastery.

11. Student rewards.

Appendix A

Student Grouping Techniques

To assure successful group activities and to provide each student an opportunity to maximize his/her potential, academic group selection must be based on specific criteria. Group selection must also directly relate to your objectives.

The following lists reflect numerous methods for grouping students. These grouping processes add variety and fun to the school day.

Name Tags

Name tags allow you to form either heterogeneous or homogeneous groups carefully, without calling unwanted attention to the reasons underlying your selection (academic levels, social skill development, etc.)

1. Choose an identifying number, letter, or name for each group and determine the work location for each group.

2. Make a sign to identify each group and place it at the appropriate workspace.

3. Write each student's name on a tag and lay the tags out in the groups you are forming. This will help you visualize the groups. Just like a hostess working out a seating arrangement for a dinner party, you can shuffle the tags around until you have a grouping that seems that it will work best for your objectives.

4. When you've decided on the composition of each group, write that group's identifying symbol on the student members' name tags.

5. Give each student his name tag and tell the class that everyone should go to the workspace or table with the symbol (letter, name, etc.) that matches the one on his own name tag.

For preschool and primary-age students, you might want to use color codes, pictures, or other symbols on the tags instead of names. You could also use paper hats made by you or your students.

Wall Charts

Write the names of students, by group, on a wall chart or chalk-board as in the sample below, and point out the location in your room where each group should assemble. If time permits, you could have students choose a name for their group as their first task.

Sample Wall Chart

Group 1: Bright Idea
Mellissa
Jenna
Joshua

Group 2: Willits' Wonders
Suzanne
Jason
Sara

Group 3: Rancho Tops
Cindy
Michael
Jamie

Group 4: Chino's Greats
Cleo
Clarence
Tom

Group 5: Sunny Sides
Marge
Billie Jo
Anthony

Group 6: Sarasota Tigers
Billy
Kathy
Robert

Group 7: Dolphins
Gregory
Pat
Jason

Group 8: Surfers
Madeleine
Tommy
Helene

Group 9: Lions
Heath
Jose
Midge

Group 10: Co-Ops
Kim
Roberto
Jan

Mystery Envelopes

You'll need an envelope for each student. You'll also need a selection of small objects.

1. Write the name of each student on an envelope.

2. As in the name tag method, sort the envelopes into groups.

3. Place the same object or assortment of objects inside the envelopes of students belonging to the same group. For example, place a paper clip in the envelope of each student belonging to Group #1; a piece of chalk inside the envelope of each student belonging to Group #2; a piece of chalk and a paper clip inside the envelope of each student belonging to Group #3; etc.

4. Seal the envelopes.

When you distribute the envelopes to your students:

1. Tell them to feel the contents of their envelopes; they may not open the envelopes, they can only "feel" what's inside.

2. Also tell them how many other students have envelopes with the same contents. If you've prepared for groups of three, for instance, you could say, "Two other students have envelopes exactly like yours. Your task is to find them. When all three of you are together, find a place in the room and sit down together."

3. Students should then open their envelopes to be sure they are really in the correct group.

Like-Sounds

1. Decide how many groups you will have and who will be in each group.

2. On 3 x 5 index cards, write the name of the same animal (examples: horse, dog, cat, owl, sheep, cow) or the same title of a song (examples: "Twinkle, Twinkle Little Star;" "Baa, Baa Black Sheep;" "Happy Birthday to You") for students who are to be in the group.

3. Distribute the cards, being sure that students you want grouped together receive the same animal or song title.

4. Students find their group members by walking around the room making the sound of the animal or humming the song. As one student finds another making the same sound, they become a pair and walk around together continuing to make their animal sound or humming their song until they have found the rest of their group.

5. When all students have located their group members, direct them to a work location.

Methods of Random Group Selection

Random selection of groups is most appropriate for non-academic activities. Groups can also be randomly selected when ability levels are nonessential to the task.

1. MYSTERY ENVELOPES

The process is the same as mystery envelopes described in the previous section with one difference — you do not write student names on the envelopes.

2. COUNTING OFF

1. First, decide how many students you want in each group. Divide that number into your total population. The result is the "count off" number.

Example: You want to have groups of four students each and you have 28 students. Going around the class, you would count off from 1 – 7. (You could have the students count themselves or you could do the counting.)

You would then tell and show each number where to gather, e.g. all the 1's sit in the right back corner of the room, all the 2's by the pencil sharpener, etc. OR you can place numbered signs at selected workspaces in the room and tell students to gather at the number that matches theirs.

Since we aren't always lucky enough to have evenly divided groups, add the one, two, or three additional students to other groups; thus, you will have groups of four with one to three groups of five.

2. Another way to count off is to determine how many students you want in each group and simply count off that many students, i.e. count one, two, three, four – these four students are a group, and so on until all students are grouped.

3. SELF GROUPING BY CATEGORY

Sometimes a bit of controlled chaos is a welcomed breather. This method is a good one for such times. It also gives students an element of choice in forming groups while insuring a good "mix-up".

Tell students to sort themselves into groups of four, or whatever size group you want to form. Each group must have at least one member who represents one of a list of categories; for example, each group must have someone:

1. wearing shoes with laces

2. with brown hair

3. wearing blue

4. born out of the state

It's okay to have a person who fits more than one criterion but all criteria must be represented in each group. If one person does fit more than one criterion, then there could be persons in the group who don't fit any of the categories.

Groups are then directed to their workplace.

4. LINE FORMATION

This method is really a variation of the "count-off" method.

Students are instructed to form a line.

Then you simply count off to the group size you want. For example, for groups of three, beginning with the first student in line, you would say, "1, 2, 3, you're a group. I'd like you to sit at the table by the door." After these students are seated, continue the process until all students have been grouped and seated.

5. THE BIRTHDAY LINE

(This group selection method was developed by Dr. Stanley Schainker from San Francisco and is used with his permission.)

Have students arrange themselves according to the month and date of their birthdays. Begin by asking who was born in January and help the January group discover who has the earliest birth date.

This student is first in line.

Direct her to stand in a specific spot in the room.

Then help students discover who has the last birthday in December and direct that student to stand at a spot that will be last in line.

Other students should then correctly arrange themselves in a line between the identified first and last students according to the month and date of their birthdays.

Once the line is formed, conduct a check by having each student, in turn, identify the month and date of their birthdays.

Count off to form groups.

6. ALPHABET LINE

Students are to arrange themselves in alphabetical order according to first name (or surname, if you prefer, or for diversity). Some groups may need visual cues. If this is true for your students, name tags can be used.

As in the Birthday Line, help students determine who will be first and last in line and tell these students where to stand.

NOTE: Other ideas for line arrangement include: height, shoe size, and distance between home and school.

The Color Spectrum

This is a good method to use when selecting groups for art projects.

Begin by reviewing a color spectrum chart, if you have one. If not, you could write the names of colors on the chalkboard. Have students arrange themselves according to the color of socks, shirts, or some other article of clothing. (In schools where uniforms are worn, consider using colored name tags.)

Subject Area Selection

Best for projects in which you want a heterogeneous mix of students and where group size can vary somewhat, such as an art collage project in which each group will bring pictures related to specific subjects for inclusion in the collage.

In this example, you would designate areas in the room for each subject or element in the collage, and have students stand by the area in which they'd like to work.

It's very possible to have many students who want to work with a specific subject area and no students wanting to work in

146

another area. If this should happen, divide the large groups into smaller groups, and eliminate the subject area in which no one has an interest to work.

Common Characteristics

First, teacher selects a common element by which students will self-select groups. Common elements are such things as hair, shoes, socks, nails, color of clothes, etc. In other words, a common element is something we all have.

Next, instruct students to group themselves in groups of (however many you've decided is best for the activity) by discovering common qualities within the element or characteristic you've selected.

For example: You want groups of 4 and students must group themselves according to the common element of shoes. Students may establish a group based on the color of shoes, that all their shoes have laces (or don't have laces), that they all have the same style shoe and so on. Students select the specific characteristic of shoes by which they will group themselves.

If groups do not work out evenly according to qualities or characteristics, it is the students' responsibility to regroup until they are in groups of 4 with each member of the group possessing the characteristic.

NOTE: Classes seldom are evenly divisible by a specific number so there may need to be one or two groups of five.

Appendix B

Awards and Forms

CERTIFICATE OF ACHIEVEMENT

Presented to:_____

on this date:_____

For outstanding performance in:

_____

Signed:_____

GOOD WORK AWARD

TO: _____

FOR: _____

_____

_____

Outstanding Award to:

_____

Because

_____

I Appreciate

_____

Because _____

_____

_____

Outstanding Achievement
as a cooperative person
AWARD

to:

_____

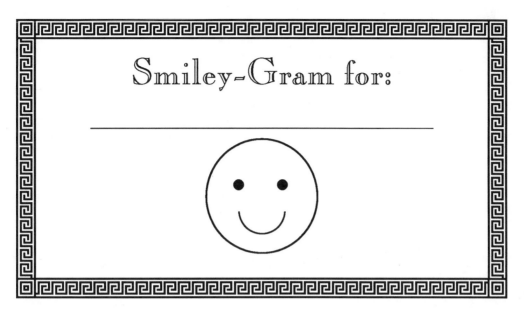

Smiley-Gram for:

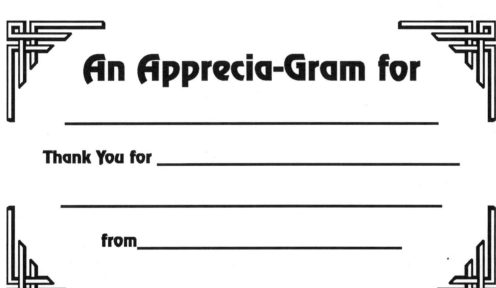

An Apprecia-Gram for

Thank You for

from

DO YOU HAVE AN IDEA TO SHARE?

The Cooperative Classroom: Social and Academic Activities is one of the many publications produced by the National Educational Service. Our mission is to provide you and other leaders in education, business, and government with timely, top-quality publications, videos, and conferences.

We are always looking for high-quality manuscripts that have practical application for educators and others who work with youth. If you or one of your colleagues has a new, innovative, or especially effective approach to some timely issue such as curriculum development, professionalism in education, teaching excellence, or some other aspect of education, please let us know.

We would like to hear from you. If you have any questions or comments about this or any of our other publications or services, please contact us. Tell us that reading this book gave you the incentive to contact us.

Nancy Shin, Director of Publications
National Educational Service
1610 West Third Street
P.O. Box 8
Bloomington, IN 47402
1-812-336-7700
or
1-800-733-6786

NEED MORE COPIES?

Need more copies of this book? Want your own copy? If so, you can order additional copies of *The Cooperative Classroom: Social and Academic Activities* by using this form or by calling us TOLL FREE at 1-800-733-6786.

We guarantee complete satisfaction with all of our materials. If you are not completely satisfied with any NES publication, you may return it to us within 60 days for a full refund.

	Quantity	Total Price
The Cooperative Classroom: Social and Academic Activities ($19.95 each) (Price is guaranteed through June 30, 1992.)	_____	_____
Shipping: Add $1.50 per copy (There is no shipping charge when you *include* payment with your order)		_____
Indiana residents add 5% sales tax		_____
TOTAL		_____

❏ Check enclosed with order   ❏ Please bill me
❏ Money Order   ❏ VISA or MasterCard

Account No._____ Exp. Date _____

Cardholder _____

SHIP TO:

Name_____Title _____

Organization _____

P.O.#_____

Address _____

City _____

State_____ ZIP_____

Phone Number _____

MAIL TO:
National Educational Service
1610 W. Third Street
P.O. Box 8
Bloomington, IN 47402